eng@gement

eng@gement

TRANSFORMING DIFFICULT RELATIONSHIPS AT WORK

LEE G. BOLMAN

JOAN V. GALLOS

WILEY

Published by John Wiley & Sons, Inc., Hoboken, New Jersey.
Published simultaneously in Canada.

For general information about our other products and services, please contact our Customer Care Department within the United States at (800) 762-2974, outside the United States at (317) 572-3993, or fax (317) 572-4002.

Wiley publishes in a variety of print and electronic formats and by print-on-demand. Some material included with standard print versions of this book may not be included in e-books or in print-on-demand. If this book refers to media such as a CD or DVD that is not included in the version you purchased, you may download this material at http://booksupport.wiley.com. For more information about Wiley products, visit www.wiley.com.

ISBN 978-1-119-15083-1 (cloth); ISBN 978-1-119-15088-6 (ePDF);
ISBN 978-1-119-15089-3 (ePub)

Printed in the United States of America.

10 9 8 7 6 5 4 3 2 1

This book is dedicated to all who have known organizational pain and injustice and who remain committed to turning around destructive workplace dynamics.

The time is always right to do what is right.

—*Martin Luther King*

CONTENTS

Contents

Contents

PREFACE

TROUBLED RELATIONSHIPS, PEOPLE PROBLEMS, AND problem people are a ubiquitous challenge of life in families, groups, and organizations. Failed relationships produce angst and wasted effort. They leave people feeling frustrated and helpless, wishing they knew better ways to respond to a chronic source of distress. At work, it could be a problem employee, a bully boss, or a constantly complaining co-worker. Beyond work, it might be a mean-spirited neighbor or a troublesome relative. We, our students, and our clients all have stories to tell—many worthy of a TV mini-series for their power and pathos. As authors, educators, and scholars long-committed to the study of organizational effectiveness, we know from deep experience the power of relationships for good or ill. We have experienced the excitement and joy of relationships characterized by trust, respect, support, and caring—and have seen the collaboration, growth, and productivity they foster. We have also known the pain and misery of relationships that undermine best practices, erode confidence, and block us from doing the things we most care about.

In an earlier work, we included a chapter on "Leading Difficult People,"[1] and many readers told us it was one of the most useful and important parts of the book. They encouraged us to look deeper, write more, and help them acquire the skills and deeper understandings needed to transform difficult relationships into productive partnerships. We appreciated their feedback, and we listened. This book is for them—and for all who struggle to turn around destructive workplace dynamics.

Search the Internet for "bad bosses," "managing difficult people," or "people problems at work," and you will encounter an almost endless stream of books, articles, websites, and blogs. [We identify some of the best in our notes.] It takes very little time to verify this as a topic that has garnered an enormous amount of attention. We learned much from studying the existing literature and resources—and from some powerful ethnographic fieldwork—and understand better why many find existing resources less helpful than intended.

Too often the advice focuses on fixing whatever is wrong with someone else—the personality flaws, obnoxious behavior, character defects, or psychopathology that make some individuals impossible to live and work with. At first glance, deep change in your difficult person may seem like the obvious solution, but that usually turns out to be mission impossible. Few managers are trained mental health professionals—and even those who are lack the time, mandate, and platform from which to facilitate the complex personal development interventions that would likely be needed. Deep personal change only comes when someone recognizes the need for it and commits to all that it takes.

Playing amateur psychiatrist also courts disaster, leading you to step into more than you are prepared to handle. Some personality types cannot deal with the reality of a mirror being held up before them. You may set off an unanticipated wave of rage, aggression, and blame aimed at you or others. It can be intellectually satisfying to confirm, for example, that you work for a skilled narcissist[2] who cannot accept disagreement, is interpersonally exploitive, sucks up and pounds down, and lacks capacity for true empathy; but that clarity may help less than you might hope. It may even exacerbate your stress and feelings of hopelessness while providing little guidance about what to do beyond run away as fast as you can.

Advice to fix someone else also puts the emphasis on the wrong place. Human behavior always happens in a social context. Blaming others or finding a scapegoat is tempting, but too often oversimplifies the problem and steers us in the wrong direction. Sometimes bad systems bring out the worst in good people, and clarifying roles and ground rules can have immediate and seemingly miraculous impact on individual behavior. That's worth remembering.

We believe a better approach emphasizes relationships, learning, imagination, and engagement. That is what this book is all about. It offers a four-step model organized around the acronym SURE: when facing a difficult people problem, you want to follow these four *rules of engagement:*

Stop, look, and learn.

Unhook.

Revise the script.

Engage your difficult person—evolve or exit.

The SURE acronym makes the basic ideas easy to remember, and we have worked to distill a complex set of issues into a framework useful across a range of situations and grounded in research and best practices. When skillfully applied, we know it works—empowering you to see more (and more clearly), embrace new options for yourself and your organization, and strengthen your confidence and impact. The four rules provide a road map to guide you through the twists and turns of challenging relationships.

A road map, however, only helps if you know how to use it, and that's where our leadership story comes in. We introduce the SURE basics in the *Introduction.* We then offer a universal leadership tale about a manager named Vicky, entering a new work situation that looks nearly impossible—a failing operation, a troubled team, and a boss from hell. All that Vicky faces could be a recipe for failure; but she is smart, savvy, patient, and courageous. The story allows you to watch Vicky at work, see how she thinks and uses advice from others, and explore the impact of what she does and says. Our leadership tale also provides specific examples of how each of the SURE principles can be successfully applied across a range of relationship difficulties and everyday managerial challenges. The book is organized to go back and forth between Vicky's story and *Interludes* that illuminate key lessons as you go along. An *Epilogue* summarizes the model.

We have not forgotten the request from our readers, clients, and students for skill building help and guidance. That's where the *Skills of Engagement Tutorial* at the end of the book comes in. It offers a deeper dive into the foundational interpersonal skills at the heart of the SURE model, along with selected references and resources for further study, and suggested exercises and activities to strengthen your people skills.

Read, enjoy, and learn! Ask others to join you in your study. Develop support groups to sustain you in challenging times. Learning to work more effectively with difficult people is a set of skills that everyone needs for success. May this volume be a source of wisdom, skill building, and strength in all you do.

INTRODUCTION

THE RIME OF THE ANCIENT MARINER[1] TELLS of a sailor who bears the curse of an albatross—a giant seabird—wrapped around his neck. He escapes this burden only when he becomes more open to the world and himself. When you find yourself at wit's end looking for some way to cope with a difficult person in your life, you've met your albatross. Like the mariner, cursing the bird or bending under its weight will only keep you adrift. The way out begins with *engagement:* finding ways to see more (and more clearly), identify new possibilities, and appreciate the benefits—even the beauty—in learning to navigate the rough waters. This deep engagement is sustained by a commitment to sort out all you face, and confidence that you've got what it takes to reach a safe harbor.

This book will help you develop the skills and strategies you need to cope with difficult relationships. Think about how you currently deal with the unusually prickly, taxing, or toxic folks who block progress, undermine your confidence, leave chaos in their wake, and cause a disproportionate share of headaches and sleepless nights. Like black holes, these difficult people suck up too much time and energy as you (and often others) struggle to live and work productively with them. They might come in the form of a problem employee, bully boss, chronically complaining coworker, mean-spirited associate, Machiavellian teammate, or troubled colleague. We all have stories to tell that end badly because we find ourselves at our worst in dealing with those who give us the hardest time. How well did you handle the last person who drove you up a wall? Did you achieve what you hoped? Did the relationship get better or worse? Were you able to alter behaviors that were destructive to individuals and to the organizations or projects that you love? If the outcomes were disappointing, this book is for you. It will show you how to engage your albatross productively and confidently.

The book advocates that deeply engaging self, other, and the situation is the best route to transform difficult relationships. It draws from two basic premises:

1. People always have more options for handling difficult situations than they recognize.
2. The stress and frustration in difficult relationships limit the ability to see and appreciate better possibilities.

Engagement leads to choices beyond fight or flight! It is always challenging, but deep engagement gets easier when you have a workable framework to guide you.

The book is built around a simple parable that illustrates four basic *rules of engagement* for staying alert, grounded, and productive in the face of difficult relationships. The story is a universal tale about life in an organization for a new manager who has inherited a group of challenging coworkers and a situation in need of a turnaround. We'd all like to live and work with perfect people, but reality doesn't always deliver our work or life mates to order. We need to cope—and thrive—with the demands of the different relationships and interpersonal styles that come our way. Difficult people are costly to organizations and toxic to those around them, and undoing their negative impact can deliver more value than hiring a superstar performer.[2] Handling difficult people takes a combination of strategy, confidence, determination, and skill. This book offers ways to enhance competencies in each of these key areas.

It tells the story of a seasoned manager, Vicky, as she copes with the cast of difficult characters she finds in her new job, seeks ways to do the work she's been hired to do, and enlists the support of her mentor and former boss, Peter. Vicky's choices and Peter's suggestions illustrate best practices and the skills needed to implement them.

Interludes periodically punctuate the story to encourage reflection and underscore key lessons for putting the four *rules of engagement* into practice. We close the book with a *Skills of Engagement Tutorial* section for those who want more *how-to* instruction on challenging fundamentals like skilled candor, mobilizing healthy support, giving and receiving feedback, testing, high quality inquiry, generating options under duress, and enhancing resilience.

Our story is set in a workplace, but you can apply its teachings wherever you need them. At its core, solving difficult people problems involves an informed approach for knowing when and how to *fix or fold*—invest in making things better or recognize it is time for someone to move on. This book shows you how.

Our approach is different from many other *how-to* books on the topic that ask readers to become amateur psychologists in order to diagnose which syndrome or psychopathology they are encountering in a boss or coworker. Is s/he a paranoid or an obsessive-compulsive? A narcissist or a histrionic? An exploder or a staller? A sniper or a know-it-all? We see several problems with that way of framing the issue.

It can lead you to make superficial or wrong judgments about troublesome people, labeling them instead of doing real diagnostic work about the full situation. Second, that approach typically leads to a diagnosis that cannot be shared. If you believe that someone is, say, a paranoid, you will likely keep that diagnosis to yourself, so it becomes undiscussable and untestable. Finally, that way of framing the issue reinforces the comfortable assumption that problems lie in something wrong with someone else. That makes it easy to feel, "I'm OK and don't need to change; I just need to find a way to shape up the other." That path leads to frustration and disappointment more often than not.

Following Harry Stack Sullivan's argument that personality manifests itself only in interpersonal relationships,[3] we believe it is more fruitful to see people problems as embedded in social interactions. That changes the question from "how do I change the other person?" to "how can I change what I do or understand in hope of improving our relationship?" Our approach focuses on a compact set of guidelines designed to produce learning and improvement across a broad range of dysfunctional relationships.

SURE *RULES OF ENGAGEMENT*

We have built the book around four rules for fixing bad situations captured in the acronym SURE. The rules are laid out to be easy to remember—a requirement for useful knowledge. They are also deep and broad enough to provide helpful guidance for most of the difficult people problems you're likely to encounter. All are grounded in research and best practices so we know that, when applied skillfully, they work. We introduce the rules in this introduction. In later sections, we delve deeper into each and show how to use them skillfully to handle specific workplace challenges such as managing your boss, coping with bullies, learning with tenacity, or leading a diverse team. We return to probe and further explore basic building blocks of the rules in our *Skills of Engagement Tutorial* in the book's final section.

1. **Stop, Look, and Learn**

    A first step in tackling difficult people problems is to stop and identify ways to harness your strongest problem-solving self. That means quieting the inner emotional turmoil and unproductive restlessness[4] that naturally arise in challenging or stressful situations. Neuroscience reminds us that the human mind naturally defaults to rehashing the past and worrying about the future, especially when things get tough: our inner dialogues reflect the special sticking power of negative thoughts. To be at your problem-solving best, quelling the feverish firing of neurons in some parts of the brain may be as important as deliberately activating others.[5]

    Difficult people also trigger impulsive responses. They remind you of some past wrong, threat, or failure. Survival instincts kick in and cloud the deep and clear thinking you need. The result: you leap before you look, typically blaming your albatross and defaulting to either fight or flight. You can find better options when you take time to understand the situation at hand. A quiet mind gets you there.

    People are difficult because they push your buttons and generate a toxic stew of emotions like anger, fear, shame, regret,

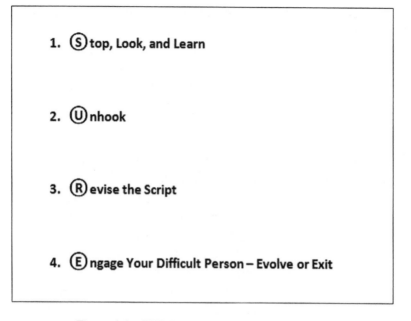

1. (S) top, Look, and Learn

2. (U) nhook

3. (R) evise the Script

4. (E) ngage Your Difficult Person – Evolve or Exit

Figure 1.1 *SURE: Four* Rules of Engagement

sadness, guilt, powerlessness, or anxiety. Acting to express or repress the feelings has a strong pull, and is also a route to bad results. It is much better to stop, acknowledge and accept the power of the impulses, and take time to see what you're up against. You'll want to look and learn about four things: (1) *individuals* (who is involved and what's happening for each person who may be contributing to this problem?); (2) *the group* (how are dynamics and interactions among members of a group creating or fueling the problem?); (3) *the system* (what's going on around you in the larger organizational environment to help create and sustain this problem?); and (4) *yourself* (what's your response, and how do you understand it?).

This four-part diagnosis is vital. You may otherwise try to solve either the wrong problem or the right problem at the wrong level. You might focus on surface disagreement, for example, when the real issues are well hidden beneath. You may point the finger of blame at an individual only to recognize too late that the problem lies in the situation rather than the person. You may see dysfunctional group dynamics as the culprit and fail to appreciate the impact of a bully boss who has everyone scurrying to meet her "my way or the highway" demands.

Multilevel diagnosis may sound daunting. It's easier if you take it one level at a time. Start by looking at the key individuals. What do you need to understand about each of them, including their history, performance, skills, needs, styles, and interests? When you believe you have the picture there, move on to thinking about the group. Ask yourself: What interpersonal and group dynamics are sustaining the current situation? How well does everyone see and understand these dynamics? Then move to the systems level: What larger situational issues, organizational history, and environmental pressures need to be understood and addressed so as to make progress?

Looking outward and around you is essential in this process. So is looking in the mirror. A relationship is a dance in which both partners contribute. As children, we learned to assign blame for every broken toy, stained carpet, or crying sibling; and it's easy in the heat of solving difficult people problems to fall back on what we know. It's also a simple way to explain anything that goes wrong, and it tells us clearly what to do next—correct, punish, or exile the guilty. But if you are a part of the problem, tossing all the blame on someone else won't accomplish much. Diagnosis requires an honest assessment of yourself. What buttons does this person push in you? Are your responses making things better or worse? Is this individual bringing out some of the worst in you? How come? What can you do about that? Understanding where you stand prepares you to tackle the next *rule of engagement*: unhook!

2. Unhook

Difficult people hook you. That's what makes them difficult. They trigger a flood of toxic emotions that makes it more likely that you'll be at your worst rather than your best. It is hard to muster clarity of thought and hope when a relationship taxes your energy and feels like an endless bog. But feeling stuck in a painful situation doesn't mean you have to stay stuck.

You can get hooked by different people at different times for different reasons—and may not even recognize what's happening to you. Difficult people may raise unresolved early life issues or dredge up a past situation that triggers automatic feelings and scripts from long ago. They may behave in ways that run counter to your core values or require responses that strain your current skill set. They may push emotional buttons you didn't know you had. Whatever the reason, if you stay hooked, you'll keep digging yourself deeper into an emotional hole. That's what makes strategies for unhooking vital. You need to know how to harness the rational part of your brain to calm your automatic physiological and emotional reactions. Regaining your sense of self-control supports the confidence and grit that help you see more clearly, strategize effectively, and make good choices.

At its simplest, unhooking is a four-step process. First, you need to recognize that you're getting hooked. Second, you need to understand the situational pattern and your triggers: what has the other person done (and in what circumstances) that has hooked you? Third, you need to identify the story you tell yourself about those kinds of situations and what that story leads you to do and feel. Fourth, you need to calm your body, mind, and heart; replace irrational and exaggerated assessments with more realistic thoughts; and change how you are reacting to the emotionally upsetting circumstances. Practices like deep breathing, exercise, relaxation techniques, practicing the virtues of gratitude and acceptance, and joyful attention training help.[6] They bolster mental strength[7] and enable better control over your emotions, thoughts, and behaviors. Once you've mastered that, you're ready to move on to the next step: revise the script.

3. **Revise the Script**

Clear, deep, and calm thinking supports your ability to write a new story that offers a different approach to your difficult person. With a new script, you can develop and rehearse alternative responses that help you try new behaviors, set boundaries, communicate more directly, and stay on task. You may be able to identify management tools (like job descriptions, contracts, or company policies) that can depersonalize challenges in the situation.[8] In the same way that professional musicians practice for hours so that muscle memory carries them through moments of forgetfulness or stage fright—and builds their confidence so that they won't be shaken if either happens— rehearsing and preparing alternative responses to difficult people increase your chances of staying grounded. Neuroscience confirms that repetition reorganizes the brain—a key for transforming new learning into expertise. In a later chapter, we'll say more about how this process works.

If you can change your script and approach, your difficult person may change as well. If you find a road closed on your way to work, you will look for another route. You may get annoyed and harbor dark thoughts about the highway department, but you'll find a new road. In the same way, if you change your actions, your difficult people may find that their old route doesn't seem to work as well anymore. They will usually try to adjust. They will learn. If not, you have learned something important about them. They may lack the ability or motivation to change. Or they may have psychological or other issues that can't be solved short of professional intervention.

The SURE model begins with finding ways to increase your agency, understanding, and capabilities. It does not set out to fix someone else. Trying to force others to change is a recipe for frustration, fights, and failure. But if you are clear and grounded, do your diagnostic diligence, and ask something different of them in return, they may adapt. You may help difficult others see better options so that their approaches to work and life bring them—and you—more success and satisfaction. The goal is win-win. They break out of unproductive ruts while you expand your leadership skills, personal resilience, and impact.

When we say people are difficult, we tend to think of them as annoying and unpleasant to be around—the kind of people Robert Sutton describes in *The No Asshole Rule*.[9] You can recognize one of those folks, Sutton says, using two clues: (1) you feel worse after spending time with the person, and (2) the individual sucks up to bosses while abusing subordinates. It's natural to want to avoid people like that, and Sutton's basic advice is, "Don't hire them in the first place." But if they're already next door or down the hall, or, even worse, you're working for one, you need to know what to do. This book teaches you that.

4. Engage Your Difficult Person—Evolve or Exit

Difficult people always present a tough choice. One option is to invest and engage with them: work deeply and earnestly to understand, repair, and strengthen the broken situation, enhancing everyone's ability to learn new ways to work better together. Another is to give up. Fix or fold? Engage or exit?

How do you decide whether it's worth the time and energy? How do you know if repair is even possible? Not every relationship works—and not everyone can succeed in every situation. It's merciful for all not to prolong shared misery. You are ahead of the game when you have clear rules for determining when it makes sense to continue to engage, how to assess if things are evolving in productive and positive ways, and when it's time for separation. *Rules of engagement* 1, 2, and 3 get you started on the right track. We'll probe other factors that can inform your decision and what to do in the face of uneven power dynamics as the book's leadership story unfolds.

HOW TO USE THIS BOOK

We have chosen to present our SURE *rules of engagement* through a leadership fable with interludes and an epilogue that underscore lessons and key points in the story. Storytelling has long been a vehicle for reflecting on human nature and the choices people make in responding to life's challenges. Storytellers paint a world of action with words. As you savor their descriptions, you slow life down: study it, think about your reactions, compare your solutions with others, and view events through multiple perspectives—your own, the writer's, and the characters in the story.

We recommend a thoughtful and deliberate read. As is always the case in human affairs, much is happening in each short exchange. As you read, compare your thinking and actions to the characters in the story. You may sometimes see the characters making mistakes that seem all too familiar. At other times, their successes may suggest new possibilities for expanding your options and becoming a better leader or collaborator. The book's power and impact depend on your ability to reflect on the issues and to use its story to better understand yourself, respond more effectively in your workplace, and handle challenges in ways that bring out the best in you and others.

Think about how you want to approach the book and how you like to learn. There are at least two paths: straight through, or story first, then interludes and lessons. If you read the book straight through, the periodic interludes offer scheduled breaks in the action for reflection and emphasis. This approach lets you cut to the chase and focus on the bottom line—what you can learn from this book. You'll digest new ideas as you go and see how they play out over the course of the story.

A second approach is to read the story itself first: skip the interludes, follow the story line, and draw your own lessons. You can reflect on what you see as most important, how well you think Vicky and others handled things, and what each of them could have done differently. This strategy keeps you focused on you—your thinking, reactions, understandings, and interpretations.

If you choose this approach, you may want to take notes as you read—what you see as most important, how you feel about each of the different characters, how you might have responded if you were in their shoes, how well you think our fictional manager is handling things, what you see as her strengths, how she uses her mentor, what you think about his advice, and so on. Then, read the six interludes. You can then compare your observations and reactions to the issues and strategies we suggest and see where we expand your thinking—or you, ours. The *Skills of Engagement* section becomes a handy reference for digging deeper into the suggested actions and strategies for success.

There's no one right way to learn from this book. Whichever approach you choose, you can benefit from reading it more than once. There's a lot packed into each scene and exchange among the characters. Take time to absorb it all. Think about what you see *really* happening and what you make of it. Notice the characters or conversations that make you most comfortable or uncomfortable. Think about times when you have been in similar situations and reflect on how you handled them. Compare your choices to what you see the characters doing—and decide what you will do differently in the future as a result.

Read. Reflect. Engage the ideas. Reread. New knowledge is only as good as your ability to use it. Find new insights into life and work situations that push your buttons. Create new responses and strategies for yourself, and try them out at work or home. Keep practicing the successful ones. Talk with others about your new plans—and about the book and what you are learning from it. Find ways to get support from others as you work to expand your relationship skills and honest feedback on how you are doing. You will build your confidence and your capabilities to handle the full range of difficult people who come your way, and model a proactive way of learning how to deal more effectively with the inevitable stresses of living and working in an increasingly complex and diverse world.

PART I

Reality

1

The Choice

VICKY SAT AT HER DESK. She opened the blue folder and reviewed the information and numbers one more time. She reread her notes from phone calls with colleagues.

I've seen the data. Know the history. Heard plenty about the players. Am I crazy to say yes to this? she asked herself. She took a deep breath and enjoyed a long, slow exhale. *Am I kidding myself to think I can turn this around?*

She'd been thinking hard since the offer on Tuesday. *I'm always up for a challenge, and this certainly counts as one*, she thought. She surprised herself when she chuckled out loud.

Vicky stared at the phone on her desk. *He's never steered me wrong before.* She picked up the receiver and dialed. She expected voice-mail, but he answered.

"Peter?"

"Vicky? Hey, what's up?"

"They've offered me the opening in Dallas, working for Michael."

"And?"

"It feels like a sinkhole. The last two people failed. They say he's impossible to work for."

"It's an opportunity."

"For what? A train wreck?"

"For proving you're even better than they think. Slaying a dragon is a great way to build a reputation."

"If the dragon doesn't get you first. This is a tough one, Peter."

"Did you get this far by playing it safe?"

"No, but not by being stupid, either."

"I've never taken a job that didn't scare me. That means I had to learn fast and stay alert to survive."

Vicky let his words sink in. Peter broke the silence.

"They think you can do it, Vicky. And if I were a betting man, I'd put my money on you. You'll learn a lot. That I guarantee."

"You're willing to field plaintive cries for help?"

"Always. More fun than a lot of things I do. And when you do well, it makes me look good."

"There's another side to that coin, you know."

"That's why I'll be here if you need me."

2

The Boss

"SO THEY PUT YOU IN the job? Dropped right at my doorstep. Well, I *am* surprised. On somebody's hot list?" His tone was cool, yet menacing. "We needed someone with experience. Someone who knows something about our products."

"I'm planning to learn. I hope I can depend on you," Vicky responded, calmly working to deflect Michael's tone and criticism.

"You'd better learn fast. That operation is the weak link in my division, and I *hate* weak links. If I didn't have so much on my plate, I'd have fixed it myself a long time ago. So get it fixed. Fast!"

"I've heard there are problems. The last two people in the job didn't make it, eh? What went wrong?" She smiled, knowing he might not like that direct question. *If Michael is my dragon,* Vicky thought, *better let him know I'm not scared—yet.*

Michael frowned and paused. He stared at Vicky. She waited: shoulders relaxed and down, smiling pleasantly.

"If I get into that, I'll have those banshees in HR breathing down my neck. I have no patience for losers. So let's just say they didn't work out and you'll have to do much, much better."

"I'm confident I can with your help."

"Oh, you'll need help, all right."

Vicky could feel herself growing tense and took a quick moment to let that go. She was expecting that her first conversation with Michael would be challenging, but the intensity of the dragon's flames was still a surprise. She tamped down the impulse to tell Michael that he was acting like a thug, that every bad thing she had heard about him must be true, and that Corporate was probably right in wondering if he was a big part of the problem. She took a deep breath instead and started again.

"What can you tell me about the team I'm inheriting, Michael?"

"Team? More like a motley crew. Bad attitudes. Big egos. Hiring mistakes. Some of 'em should have been fired long ago. Figure out how to fix that. And just make sure you make your numbers."

"I'm scheduled to meet with them this afternoon. Can you come and introduce me?"

"Can't. I'm booked. But they report to you. They'll figure out fast who you are."

"Fair enough." An image flashed across Vicky's mind. She was drowning. Michael was the lifeguard. He was staring right at her and ignoring her cries. She put that aside. "See you tomorrow?"

"I'm booked solid for the next few days or so. I'll have Sandy set up a meeting when I'm more open next week."

"Okay. See you then."

3

A Single Step

VICKY WAS CAREFUL TO SMILE and walk confidently as she headed back to her office. She knew others might be watching for signs that Michael had needed only one meeting to work his dark magic. She entered her office and deliberately left the door open.

She sat at her desk and turned to her computer. She began to make notes on the meeting with Michael. *Now I know why Michael is a legend,* she thought. *But it could have been worse.*

Vicky continued jotting down her recollections of the meeting. *I want a record even though it's a meeting I wouldn't mind forgetting.*

As Vicky wrote, she felt good about one pattern she was already seeing. Her questions had worked well as a counter to Michael's provocations. *Let's keep that in the playbook,* she told herself. She then thought about the stress and turmoil she had felt. *He's not going to make this easy.*

She paused, and let a wave of discouragement pass. *Well, as they say, with all this manure, there must be a pony somewhere. I just have to keep looking.*

Vicky was about to press *save,* but stopped. One more thought came to her, and she typed a Chinese proverb: the journey of a thousand miles begins with a single step. Vicky saved her file and turned to her e-mail.

Interlude I

Coping with Bullies

WE LEARN FROM VICKY'S CALL TO PETER that she has some of the right stuff for a successful management career: she does her homework, she's thoughtful about career decisions, she has developed and maintains strong networks and workplace relationships, and she's willing to ask for help. She's tapped her colleagues to research the Dallas job and sees that it could be a setup for failure. She recognizes that the company's offer is a mixed bag, has done her best to think through all she knows, and tests her judgment with a trusted mentor. Senior leadership wants her to step up to the plate in Dallas, and she wants to make the right career choice. She can confirm that she's a team player by accepting the challenge, but it won't help her or the company if she strikes out. With Peter's encouragement and promise of support, she concludes the opportunities outweigh the risks.

Vicky's first meeting with Michael reminds her of just how hard the challenges will be. Her image of drowning while Michael ignores her cries captures her fears and disappointment in a boss who seems willing to let her sink—or even throw her to the sharks. Michael is a classic bully, and bullies are a nightmare for everyone around them. It's even tougher when the bully is the boss. How can Vicky cope with Michael and move the relationship onto more positive and productive ground?

Bullies represent a growing and troubling workplace phenomenon.[1] Examining how Vicky handles her initial encounter with Michael provides a powerful example of how the *rules of engagement* can help in the toughest challenges. It also enables you to deepen your understanding of how to put each rule to use.

1. **Stop, Look, and Learn: Avoid the Obstacles**

   Vicky comes prepared to her first meeting with Michael with a basic strategy of stop, look, and learn. She's done enough homework to have thoughts on what might be happening in Dallas, but it's too early to lock into a diagnosis or assume that she understands it all. Vicky's plan is to ask questions and learn more. Even when Michael challenges her, she works to stay open to learning. Vicky understands that she needs Michael as an ally. He's the boss; and he has information, access, and resources that she needs. She soon learns that building an open relationship with him will not be easy, and that it will be a rough road if she has to wade through an endless stream of Michael's toxicity. His out-of-the-gate hostility surprises her, and she is now better prepared should it surface again.

   It also helps to remember that bullies are often insecure, unhappy people whose bark may be worse than their bite. That is a testable proposition. It is easier to see the importance of testing and to have patience and compassion when you see someone as a vulnerable or troubled colleague rather than an obnoxious thug. Vicky needs to stay open. It is early in her relationship with Michael, and things might improve as they become more comfortable with each other.

   But Vicky also needs to stay alert. Bullies can mistake empathy and patience for weakness or submissiveness—and nothing fuels a bully more than a weak or submissive target, especially bullies who have succeeded with a thug strategy in the past and been allowed to get away with it by their boss or organizational culture. Research tells us that people with prosocial orientations—those focused on understanding, learning, helping, seeing the best in others, making contributions to a larger good—are most at risk of becoming targets.[2]

Informed compassion needs to be Vicky's mantra going forward: assume the best until consistent data confirms otherwise. Her tension in her initial exchange with Michael is functional. It signals a need to remain vigilant, and that the risk of saying or doing the wrong thing may be high in this relationship. Vicky shows skill in attending to Michael's cues and being ready to shift strategies and directions if necessary. She makes productive use of her stress by wedding mindfulness with relaxation techniques—a proven strategy for building resilience and psychic strength.[3] A central risk in working with difficult people, especially bullies, is that emotions will take over and lead to ineffective or impulsive action.

2. **Unhook: Know the Signs**

We know from Vicky's call to Peter that she looked carefully at the Dallas assignment before agreeing to take it on. She wisely sought counsel from a trusted mentor to get his perspective on whether her experiences and skills positioned her to succeed in the challenging job. The conversation helped Vicky confirm her strengths and support base, and enter a tough situation grounded and informed. That made it easier for her not to get hooked by Michael's early provocations.

Michael greeted Vicky with a message designed to deflate and intimidate: you're unqualified, you're likely to fail, and you won't get much help from me. This is classic bully behavior: attack, threaten, and humiliate others so as to frighten them and throw them off balance. Workplace bullying takes the form of acts of commission or omission.[4] In one short exchange, Michael does both—a sign that he has played this game before and it has worked for him.

Bully behavior is both intimidating and infuriating. It sets up a dilemma between fight and flight. It's tempting to back off and let the bully have his or her way to avoid an unpleasant battle. That's what the bully is hoping for. Workplace bullying is all about control: the bully needs to establish power over those perceived as threats. But it can be even worse if your anger takes over and you launch a counterattack. Head-to-head combat with a dangerous and powerful opponent may generate gruesome battle scars—and stories that the bully can use in maintaining the upper hand or in discrediting you. Bullies sustain their power because the fight or flight reaction comes so naturally to their targets. Michael expects that others will retreat in the face of his intimidation, or lose control and do something stupid. Vicky breaks the pattern. She recognizes the feelings that Michael's behavior is generating for her. That's an important first step in unhooking. Second, she listens to the story unfolding in her head: "He *is* a thug, he's the problem here, he might be the worst boss in the world, and he's going to watch me drown." She pauses long enough to see that dwelling or acting on that story would lead nowhere good. She deliberately takes a deep breath, a simple yet proven way to disrupt the body's automatic stress response in the face of perceived danger.[5] At that point, Vicky is ready to look for a more productive story, the next step in the SURE model.

3. **Revise the Script: Advance Your Goal**

Michael's steady drumbeat of putdowns tempted Vicky to take the bait, but she shows impressive self-possession and emotional intelligence[6] in avoiding the traps he was setting. She unhooks from her rising anger and skirts the knee-jerk impulse to tell Michael he is a bad boss and worse human being. Instead, she reaffirms her goal for their exchange and switches to a more productive internal storyline: "I need to learn as much as I can from Michael and now is a good time to begin doing that." Vicky knows that she needs a productive working relationship with him, even though he is not making it easy. She demonstrates skill in staying on task.

Success in understanding the situation and in establishing a relationship with her boss will take persistence, savvy, and patience. Vicky's post-meeting notes to herself are a way to debrief a stressful exchange and provide data she can return to later to search for patterns and progress. Professional athletes review videos to study what they did well and where they can improve. Vicky's notes serve a similar purpose.

4. **Engage: Finesse, Not Force**

A key to engagement with difficult people is using finesse instead of force. This is especially true in situations of unequal power, as with a boss. Vicky is a model of finesse in her initial meeting with Michael. She responds to his "cool yet menacing" critique of her inexperience by adroitly indicating how much she hopes to learn from him and others. She employs two of the most powerful and disarming messages for dealing with anyone who can help or harm us: *I need your help* and *I want to learn from you.* When Michael tells her that her operation is hanging by a thread and has to get better fast, he's inviting her to become defensive or back off. Vicky calmly acknowledges instead the reality that her two predecessors "didn't make it," and turns the tables with the simple question, "What went wrong?" She demonstrates a principle of finesse rooted in martial arts like aikido and jiujutsu: deflect and leverage the attacker's energy rather than oppose it directly. Asking questions is a good way to do that.

Inquiry enables Vicky to begin securing the information she needs to do her job. It is also a low-risk way to engage the bully and let him know that she's not scared by his attacks. Her question, "What went wrong?" also gently confronts Michael's vulnerabilities without escalating the fight. Workplace bullies often accelerate the abuse when their targets are intimidated or unwilling to confront; but, like Michael, they are often less prepared to deal with probing questions. It is easy to under-estimate the power of skilled inquiry. Developing your ability to ask the right questions is a key skill in almost any relationship, all the more so with difficult bosses like Michael. An added benefit is that you may learn something important.

Vicky is in her first day on the job and in her first meeting with her new boss. First meetings can be fateful because both parties are forming initial impressions that can influence everything that follows. Vicky astutely attends to both the words and the music—the content of what is said, as well as the emotional subtext. Michael's substantive message is direct, "Your department is in trouble and you'd better fix it fast, even though you will probably fail because you don't have the right experience." She wisely avoids rash statements or promises that she might regret later. She also sidesteps the potential trap of trying to prove how good she is to counter Michael's questions about her experience. Vicky communicates instead that she sees Michael as a valuable resource—which he is—and that she wants a relationship built on mutual respect and working together on the shared goal of organizational turn-around. Finesse, not force.

Vicky has big challenges ahead, and things are likely to get worse before they get better. With bullies, they always do. But Vicky demonstrates her strength and confident engagement in a rough opening meeting. She'll undoubtedly face other tests, but she is off to a strong start.

PART II

Beginnings Are Everything

4

The Motley Crew

THE WOMAN WAS PROBABLY NO older than late thirties, but her close-cropped hair, plain gray suit, and buttoned-up white blouse gave the air of an aging recluse who craved invisibility. She was sitting at the far corner of the table in the meeting room, eyes glued to the laptop in front of her. She looked up as Vicky arrived. She gave Vicky a small, awkward smile, and then seemed to freeze. Vicky smiled warmly, walked around the table, and offered her hand.

"I'm Vicky. You must be Lin."

Lin nodded and raised a stiff arm for a quick handshake. No words. She had a small, frozen smile. No eye contact.

"You're the business manager, right?"

Another nod. Eyes back down.

"I'm looking forward to working with you, Lin. I expect I'll be relying on you a lot."

She waited, but Lin just nodded again. As Vicky wondered where to take the conversation next, the door opened and another woman entered. No younger than Lin, but the wavy brown hair, colorful outfit, sparkling tennis bracelet, and practiced smile conveyed energy and a carefully crafted self-presentation.

Her greeting was immediate and enthusiastic. "You must be Vicky," she said with her hand straight out for a handshake. "I'm

Madison. Director of Marketing. I speak for everyone when I say that we're all so excited to meet you. You've met Lin? She's such a treasure. We all love her. I know you will, too."

"Lin and I just met, and it's a pleasure to meet you as well, Madison. I did marketing in my last job, so I expect we'll have plenty to talk about."

"Yes. Of course. But not with our products. I'll be glad to help you learn."

"Thanks. I'm counting on that."

A murmur of male voices punctuated by bursts of laughter grew louder until their three owners came into the room, engaged in an animated conversation. When they noticed Vicky, they fell silent.

"Hi, guys. I'm Vicky."

"Who'd have guessed?" said a squat man with a ruddy complexion.

Vicky ignored his sarcastic tone. "And you are?"

"Nathan."

"Director of Engineering."

"Right."

"A pleasure to meet you," she said with an outstretched hand. "You're so important to the business."

"It's about time someone noticed."

Vicky turned to the taller man on Nathan's right. "And you're . . . ?"

"Carlos. In my second year running production."

"I'm looking forward to working with you, Carlos, and getting to know a lot more about our operations."

"Always at your service," he responded with a gentle nod and warm smile.

Vicky turned to the third man. "And you must be Gene, who sells everything that Nathan designs and Carlos makes."

"Not everything," he replied with a thinly disguised scowl. "Only the good stuff. But if anyone can move their junk, I can."

"What Gene means," said Nathan derisively, "is that every once in a while his people get lucky and trip over a customer."

Gene was about to respond, but Madison jumped in. "Oh, gentlemen, behave. We have work to do here. We need to hear from Vicky. These guys love to tease each other."

"I'm all for having fun at work," Vicky said. "And your comment, Madison, takes us right to a topic for today's meeting. How we're all going to work together. Please, sit down everyone."

Vicky watched as Madison positioned herself at the head of the table. Nathan and Gene sat on either side of her, and Carlos positioned himself between Gene and Lin. Vicky chose to sit next to Nathan and opposite the trio on the other side.

Vicky had thought long and hard about how to begin. She'd been here before—the first meeting with a new group of subordinates. *Beginnings are important*, she reminded herself. But she felt as much apprehension as excitement. Where do you start if you know your new group has a weak track record and a reputation for being tough to manage? *Well,* she'd told herself, *be positive and emphasize the possibilities—and tell the truth.*

"I have to say I feel like a kid who's just transferred to a new school. I'm hoping for a great experience but I need to learn the lay of the land, and I'm sure there'll be challenges along the way. I see tremendous upside potential for this business, and it will take all of us working hard and working together to make that happen. My hope for this meeting is that . . . ."

The door opened and slammed noisily into the wall behind it. In walked Michael.

"Trips got canceled," he said casually. "So I came by to see how you all and Vicky are getting along. I hope she told you I made it very clear that this group needs to shape up."

Vicky could not have been more surprised if Michael had motored into the room on a Harley. She hoped that she didn't look as stunned as she felt. *Take a deep breath,* she told herself, *and don't make things worse.*

"Michael," she finally said, "please join us." Vicky motioned toward the seat beside her. "We were just getting started. My agenda for the meeting is . . . ."

"I'll just sit in the back," he interrupted and noisily dragged a chair from the table to a position along the wall. He sat down and then leaned back, stretching his legs out in front of him. He crossed his arms tightly over his chest and smiled at the group. "Don't mind me. Go on. I just like seeing my people in action."

5

SOS

"I EXPECTED TO LAST MORE than a day before my first distress call," Vicky said, trying for some levity in her opening. She sat leaning over her desk, resting her head on the palm of one hand and holding the phone with the other.

"First days can be tough. Dying to hear about yours. How'd it go?"

"Murdering my boss is probably a bad career move so I need a Plan B, right?"

Peter and Vicky both laughed. She leaned back in her chair, and let herself fully feel for the first time how disappointed she was about day one in Dallas.

"Haven't we had this conversation before?" he asked.

"Which one? The downside of murdering a coworker?"

"Managing your boss 101."

"That's for normal people, Peter. Not Michael."

"How do you know unless you give him a chance?"

"That's more than he's giving me. He said he couldn't come to the first meeting with my new team. Then he showed up unannounced and did a great job of disrupting things. Should I go on?"

"Remind me what you expected it would be like to work for Michael," Peter asked kindly.

"Maddening."

"So is any of this a real surprise?"

"No. Just worse than I expected."

"Did you crumble or grovel or wail or curse?"

"No, Peter," Vicky said with a laugh.

"Then it sounds on track to me." Peter paused before continuing, giving Vicky time to remember she had handled a tough start pretty well.

Peter continued. "First time you worked for me, I said aim for three things in a relationship with a boss."

"I remember. Partnership. Open communication. Trust. None of which I have with Michael."

"You've been there how long?"

"Okay, one day," Vicky smiled ruefully. "I get the hint."

Peter was silent at the other end of the line. It was the way he often signaled that she was seeing something important.

"I know," Vicky continued, "it takes time to build a relationship with a boss. But so far we're going in the wrong direction. Fast."

"So how can you turn it around?"

"Well, thanks to you, managing your boss 101 is branded in my brain."

"Let's apply it to Michael."

"Step 1: look at myself. What's my piece of the puzzle?"

"And?"

There was a long pause. Finally, Vicky spoke.

"I should have thought of this before, but it probably didn't help that I arrived expecting the worst and wondering how I was going to survive. I'd heard so much negative stuff about Michael. Hiding it well, I hope, but it was hard to avoid confirming his faults at every turn."

"Could be a recipe for missed opportunities."

"Had him convicted in my mind before the case ever went to trial."

"That'll make it harder to walk in his shoes. Find out what's really behind that threatening mask."

"That wasn't anything I gave much thought to today." Vicky paused and then added with a sigh, "So, my good teacher, remind me: I've lost track of step 2."

"Easy to forget when you don't have the boss of your dreams." Vicky nodded as Peter spoke. "Step 2: understand the boss's problems and pressures so you can use his time wisely. Figure out how to make his life easier. He doesn't need you to be one more problem." Vicky was thinking about what might make Michael's life easier when Peter broke the silence.

"You're the third batter up to the plate, Vicky. The first two in the job struck out." Peter said, "Inning's almost over."

"Meaning?"

"Michael's got to be nervous."

"So maybe he needs me as much as I need him?"

"Bingo."

6

The Ally

SHE STOOD OUTSIDE MICHAEL'S DOOR, holding a sheet of paper. *He needs you,* she reminded herself. Vicky straightened her shoulders, stepped forward, tapped lightly, and stuck her head in the door.

"Hey, got a minute?" Vicky asked confidently and with a smile. *Talk to him the way you would Peter,* she told herself.

"Barely," Michael grumbled, not looking up from the piles of scattered papers on his desk.

"I won't take long. I've been well-trained to use my boss's time wisely."

Michael glanced up. "Well, that's something."

"I'll take that as my first compliment." Vicky pulled a chair up to the front of Michael's desk and sat directly opposite him. He looked up. Vicky caught the flicker of a brief smile. *Treat him the way you would Peter,* she repeated to herself.

"Well?"

"Michael, I took this job because I'm confident we can get this unit back on top of its game. I'm here to work hard for you and with you. I want to make both of us look good. What do you need from me to feel you can trust me?"

Michael looked up and stared at her. Vicky held his gaze and her composure. She waited.

"Start by tackling that useless crew of yours." He returned to his papers.

"My first priority. You think we have the wrong people on the bus?"

Michael's laugh sounded almost malicious. "You could fire the whole lot of them, as far as I'm concerned. Just make sure you make your numbers."

"I plan to beat the numbers," Vicky said calmly. Then she placed a short outline of what she planned to do on Michael's desk. "Here's my proposed strategy going forward. Basically, you'll see I'm meeting with everyone, assessing what they can contribute, and testing whether they really want to be on the team. I'd like your thoughts on the plan. Did I miss anything? All suggestions welcomed."

She waited as Michael glanced at her sheet and then returned to his paperwork. After a few minutes that felt much longer to Vicky, Michael stopped writing. He opened a file drawer in his desk and pulled out a thick folder.

"Here." He threw the folder on the desk in Vicky's direction. She saw what looked like personnel files for everyone in her department.

"Thanks, Michael. This will help, I'm sure. I'll review everything."

"Well, get started." He returned to his paperwork.

Vicky stood up. "Will do, boss. It's my job to make you look good."

"That would be great if I thought you could."

"Michael, if the business does well, we both look good. And, if I help you, I'm hoping you'll help me. Fair enough?"

"Words are cheap."

"I agree. I know I have to deliver. I plan to. And it'll be easier if we're on the same team. My motto is no games and no surprises."

She turned to go.

"Hey," he called after her. "No games, no surprises, eh? I'll hold you to that."

"I hope you will."

Interlude 2

Managing the Boss

PETER REMINDS VICKY OF A TASK AS important as anything else she must do: manage her boss. Prescriptions for workplace success often emphasize managing people who report to you. Savvy professionals understand that if they can't lead up, they won't be able to lead down either. Coping with a bully is one aspect of Vicky's challenge with Michael. She also has the job that subordinates always face of how to develop a productive working partnership with a boss.

A boss's position power creates imbalances and barriers, even when the boss is warm and supportive. The trick to managing up is building a relationship of mutual influence despite the reality of unequal power. This is harder, but even more important, with bosses like Michael who see no need for a two-way street.

There are wonderful bosses and terrible ones in any line of work. Vicky does not have the boss of her dreams, but she needs to do the best she can with the one she has (at least until one of them moves on). Unless she finds a way to work productively with Michael, she is in a no-win situation. Michael has information and experience she needs, and Vicky would be foolish to underestimate his influence over resources or important others in Dallas and elsewhere. If she can't meet his expectations, she looks weak and ineffective. If she lets him walk over her, she doesn't help her career, her health, or the business.

Despite what cynics might think, managing up does not amount to self-serving manipulation or becoming a lackey. It is a strategic and orchestrated approach for developing clear expectations and communication patterns that enable you and your boss to work together on behalf of both personal and institutional goals. The support of those above you makes it easier to get the resources you need, projects you enjoy, and opportunities you want for advancement. It provides cover when you are under attack—and the confidence to think long term and to take risks on behalf of your unit's mission and your career development. Without support from above, your wings are clipped—whether you realize it or not.

If you are blessed with a wise and supportive boss, nurture that relationship. Vicky is fortunate that somebody up there likes her. She has a mentor in Peter, and the offer of Dallas from Corporate means that there are also others interested in her growth and advancement. But no one can do her work for her. She still has to find a way to move her relationship with Michael on to a more positive footing. His responses to her best efforts provide important data to assess what works and what's possible. Waiting for Michael to change or to reach out is an abdication of her leadership: Vicky needs to be proactive. Wherever you work, if you want your job and want to do it well, you need a strategy for working effectively with your boss.

So what do you do if, like Vicky, you have a dominating, uncommunicative boss like Michael? Let our *rules of engagement* be your guide.

1. Stop, Look, and Learn: Understand the Boss's Problems and Be a Solution

Vicky recognizes that she needs to understand Michael's pressures, problems, and working style. She is busy and Michael is probably even busier, so she wants to maximize the value of the time they spend together. That means using it on the things that are important to both of them. To learn about Michael's needs and priorities, Vicky understands that she has to take initiative rather than hope for him to volunteer. She knows that Michael has goals to achieve, hasn't been successful with her two predecessors, and may face pressures and constraints she doesn't know about. Understanding Michael's agenda and concerns will help her gauge how she could make his life easier. Demanding, needy, or oblivious subordinates tend to have a short shelf life, even for the most patient and nurturing of bosses. Michael's bullying adds difficulty and urgency for Vicky. He needs to see her as a valuable asset, and achieving agreed-upon goals is a good way. But she also needs to stay alert to the possibility that the more she succeeds, the more threatened Michael may feel.

Vicky also needs to understand how Michael prefers to communicate so that she can deliver messages in a format that works for him. In her SOS conversation with Peter, she recognizes that her concerns about Michael's track record may be getting in her way. Seeing Michael as dangerous can mobilize a desire to keep a safe distance. Vicky needs to lean in and get close if she really wants to learn about Michael's problems and pressures. If she doesn't, she will never understand why he is thinking and acting as he does—or have much hope of influencing either. You can understand much about difficult people when you replace your fears with sincere interest and allow yourself to walk in their shoes. That's not easy with a bully boss like Michael, but you cannot test the potential in a relationship without making an effort.

2. **Unhook: Employ Mindful Vigilance**

We see from Vicky's phone call to Peter that despite best efforts in her initial meeting with Michael she ends up feeling hooked. Michael's surprise visit to her team meeting tipped the scale. It's the one specific example she shares with Peter, and her reference to needing a Plan B illustrates its impact. Talking with Peter helps Vicky sort through what worked and what didn't in a dramatic day one. A supportive mentor or coach is a valuable asset.[1]

The plethora of books about bad bosses[2] tells you something: lots of people have worked for one—or thought they did. Bad bosses run the gamut from ineffective to unethical, and the list of most common types is sobering: incompetent, callous, corrupt, rigid, intemperate, insular, and evil leaders.[3] When it happens to you, look for the pattern that can help you unhook:

what is the boss doing that raises your angst, what story are you telling yourself about it, and what button does that push in you? A good analysis gets you clearer on what you might do differently. If Vicky simply folds or balks, she will not get what she needs from Michael and he won't learn anything about his own effectiveness. That's no favor to either of them. Michael continues a pattern of unintentionally digging himself into deeper leadership holes, and Vicky races toward burnout.

From her first meeting with Michael, Vicky looks to understand and to unhook from the powerful emotions that he triggers for her so that she can be at the top of her game. Unhooking is almost never one and done. Vicky will need to make it an ongoing focus of her attention.

3. **Revise the Script: Meet the Subordinate Challenge**

Vicky sees that her internal script kept her guarded and focused on Michael's past transgressions. That frees her to develop an approach to their second meeting that focuses on speaking warmly and genuinely to his concerns—something Michael might not expect, given his cantankerous behaviors to date. Early in the meeting, for example, Vicky promises to use his time efficiently and announces her goal of making them both look good. Vicky has wisely tossed out the script that subordinates often use with difficult bosses—be cautious and let the boss make the decisions. Instead, she presents her proposed plan and asks Michael for feedback.

Speak Up. One of the most common barriers to communication with one's boss is the fear of speaking up. Bosses are not infallible, and they are not well served by subordinates who hesitate to tell the truth about the potential fallout from their judgments and decisions. A key leadership capacity is the willingness to speak truth to power and the ability to do it with grace and skill. Subordinates sometimes fail this test because they cannot overcome their fear of the consequences. And attacks, blame, and reckless personal insults are unproductive. Contrary to conventional wisdom, though, skilled candor delivered with genuine concern for the enterprise—and the boss—can increase one's credibility and influence. If it does not, you have learned something very important about your boss. Beware!

Offer solutions, not problems. Too often, subordinates turn to their bosses with the explicit or implicit message, "Tell me what you want me to do." If bosses take the bait, the result is usually a disempowered subordinate and an overloaded boss. It is better to take responsibility and make your boss's job easier, not harder. It is wise to consult with bosses on issues that might wind up on their desks anyway, but they are likely to be grateful and to have more confidence in you if you arrive with thoughtful solutions and progress reports. When your implicit message is "Solve this problem for me," you raise red flags about your initiative and strategic capabilities. When you say, "Here's what I see. Here's what I've done. Here's what I've learned. And here's my plan. Any advice?" you keep your boss in the loop without putting one more problem on the boss's plate. That is just what Vicky does when she presents her planning document to Michael and asks for his reactions.

4. **Engage: Sustain Your Diagnostic Eye**

Peter identifies three overarching goals for a productive boss-subordinate relationship, the first of which is partnership. A partnership is a cooperative venture with mutual objectives. That won't be easy with a boss like Michael, but it is not impossible. Building a partnership requires conversation and shared agreement about roles, goals, expectations, and assessment standards. Working through those issues, especially if there are major differences in perspectives, enables both parties to emerge with a stronger sense of trust and appreciation of the mutual benefits of the relationship.

The ideal time to begin that conversation is before you accept the job, but it is never too late to start. The objective is to clarify what each of you needs from the other. Vicky, for example, needs things like information, counsel, support, protection, resources, and clear mandates from Michael. He needs information, support, accountability, integrity, and reliable performance from Vicky. Smart subordinates understand that it's all about reciprocity: you deliver for your boss, and your boss is more likely to do the same for you.

At the center of Vicky's approach to Michael in their second meeting is an offer she hopes he won't refuse: if we can be partners, I'll make you look good. Michael, chronic curmudgeon that he is, is skeptical and not yet ready to sign on. But he doesn't say no, and gives indications that he is intrigued. In response, he makes his first gesture of support: the personnel files. Vicky ignores the brusque way the files are tossed in her direction. She chooses instead to thank Michael for sharing them. She expresses her genuine appreciation for the information, confirms her intention to use it, and manages the whole exchange as an opportunity to reinforce her commitment to partnership. Vicky's cheerful tenacity and focus on task may be starting to pay off.

Peter's second overarching goal for a productive boss-subordinate relationship is open communication. Not easy with someone like Michael, but Vicky still needs to find ways to communicate with him so that they understand each other. She improves her chances by working to see the world through his eyes so she can position her ideas and suggestions in light of his needs. Michael may not yet appreciate that working closely with Vicky is in his best interest, but Vicky can show him why it is. If she doesn't and things go downhill, he'll blame her anyway.

As in her previous meeting with Michael, Vicky asks good questions. She also makes it clear that she wants Michael's advice and input. Her skillful use of questions gives her a way to take initiative without offending Michael or offering him new openings for attack. When speaking up seems risky, it is a good time for *inquiry*. You can argue directly with some bosses; it's futile with others. But asking the right questions often accomplishes the same result.

A good example is Vicky's question to Michael, "What do you need from me to feel you can trust me?" She puts trust on the table in a way that lets Michael respond on his terms. Good questions help Vicky understand Michael's thinking, and they stimulate him to think again.

Peter's third goal is to establish the credibility needed to negotiate key priorities with your boss. Credibility is built on competence and trust. You may have solid experience and business acumen, but if people don't trust you as the messenger, they won't trust your message. Leaders build their credibility when they consistently demonstrate their integrity and reliability in achieving or exceeding their stated objectives. Bosses trust and listen to employees who have their best interests at heart: making your boss look good is a proven formula for success in any organization. That can even work with Michael—looking good may be high on his list of priorities.

Vicky is sufficiently confident and determined to take the risk of making a series of commitments that respond to Michael's needs—she'll meet or beat her numbers, solve the personnel issues, and work to make him look good. Avoiding commitments for fear that you won't meet them is a route to mediocre performance. Vicky understands that she's putting her credibility on the line, and that she'll need to make good on those promises. She offers only what she knows she can deliver. Be forewarned: credibility may take time to build, and it can be quickly lost.

Vicky's promise of "no games and no surprises" shows Michael that she understands the importance of not letting him be blind-sided. Subordinates often make the mistake of withholding bad news in the hope that they'll get it resolved before the boss hears about it—or even cling to the magical thinking that it will somehow go away. Wise subordinates understand that if there's an issue in their area that could produce an explosion, create problems upstairs or with customers, or generate negative press, they need to alert their boss immediately. They want the boss to understand the issues, know the risks, and, ideally support whatever they're going to do to deal with the problem at hand. It may go without saying, but it can't be said too often: all your choices should be clear, clean, and ethical.

Vicky is wise to stay alert, debrief periodically with Peter, and continue recording notes for reflection and patterns.

Michael has shown classic bully behaviors. Like abusive spouses, bully bosses like to keep their targets close yet off-balance by using periods of peace and apparent progress as a way to dangle hope for a better relationship. Then, whack![4] Michael needs numbers that make Vicky's operation in Dallas look good, but that does not mean he'll be delighted if she accomplishes what he has been unable to do to date. It may seem counterintuitive, but workplace bullies do not usually target incompetent people. They are threatened by capable, courageous, and well-liked individuals who do, know, and get things they can't. So workplace bullies look for ways to get free agents under control, and often coax or coerce allies to help in that effort.[5]

Vicky walks a fine and difficult line: she cannot be naïve, nor can she write her boss off after a few exchanges and still do the work she needs to do. Her perspective and skill may turn things around with Michael. If not, she will at least know that she gave it her best shot. Vicky will draw strength and insight by continuing to define herself as an empowered learner. She also needs to remember that signs of progress with Michael do not ensure a durable peace. Michael may still resort to subtle or devious means to control and undermine her. Bully bosses make the power differences and complexities in boss-subordinate relationships much more difficult. But openness and hope can coexist with vigilance, self-care, and smart diagnostic work.

PART III

Complex Characters

7

Madison

VICKY EMBARKED ON HER PLAN. Her next step was to meet with each of her people individually: get their thinking, probe their views on the group's disappointing track record, and work to develop agreement about how to go forward. She asked each of them to find a convenient time to meet. Vicky wasn't surprised that Madison, her marketing manager, was first to sign up.

Madison welcomed Vicky with the mannered enthusiasm of a veteran marketer. She was on her feet, big smile, hand outstretched, as Vicky entered Madison's office. Madison's tone was enthusiastic. "Vicky, thanks so much for coming over to marketing central."

"My pleasure," Vicky responded, as she took in the colorful riot of memorabilia and photos spread over the walls and work surfaces in Madison's office. They conveyed the image of a celebrity—a smiling, self-possessed, stylish woman who always seemed to be at center stage. "Your office has a lot of character," Vicky added.

"Thanks. That means *so* much to me. I hope it shows how important my work is to me and the company. But I know you didn't come here to talk about my decorating panache. You want to talk about how we can improve the business."

"Exactly," Vicky interjected.

"I can't tell you how happy I am to work with you, and I really want to help in any way I can."

"I appreciate that, Madison. I'm sure you're aware that the group's business results have been disappointing, and we need to fix that."

"Well, we've had some problems, but it's nothing that we can't fix."

"So," asked Vicky, "where should we start?"

"Do you want me to be honest?"

"Absolutely."

Madison walked over to close her door before returning to her seat.

"I just hate to say anything negative about my colleagues, but you've asked for the truth, and I want to make sure you have the full picture."

"I appreciate that."

"I feel I can be honest with you, Vicky," said Madison, in a soft, conspiratorial tone. "I've done my best to hold this group together in the last couple of years, but it's been a struggle. I'm sure you know you're here because your predecessors couldn't do the job. Part of that is Michael isn't easy to work for. But, frankly, I think their biggest problem was that they couldn't face the awful truth."

Madison paused.

"What truth?" Vicky asked calmly.

"Oh, this is so hard for me to say," said Madison with a frown. She paused, closing her eyes and putting her head down.

Vicky waited until Madison began again.

"I guess I just have to say it. They didn't have the guts to fire people who needed to go."

"Why do you say that?" Vicky asked, again in a calm voice.

"I look at it from a marketing perspective. My job as a marketer is to give our customers what they want. We're not doing that."

"Why not?"

"I know what we need to put out there, and I've spent a lot of time trying to bring my colleagues along to see things my way. But it's been slow and painful—worse than pulling teeth."

"Because?" Vicky nudged.

"Okay. Nathan is brilliant. Great engineer. But he's never met a new idea he thinks will work. Every glass is half empty for Nathan, and he's so testy. You never know when he'll be in a bad mood. So I cajole and nudge and suggest and then cajole some more. Sometimes, he'll come around to see things my way. He knows I know my stuff. Once he buys in to a new idea, his group does a great job. But it's *so* hard to get him there. And the process takes so long that we're constantly late to market."

"Okay. So one thing we have to do is speed up our product development cycle?"

"Right. But that'll only help if we can make it once it's designed."

"Why do you say that, Madison?" Vicky asked.

"I just hate to say this, Vicky, but Carlos is in over his head. He can't admit it and no one else will either. Nicest guy in the world. Always means well. Up through the ranks. Knows the operations. Supports his people. But you just can't rely on him."

"So, he doesn't deliver?"

"He likes to keep people happy and doesn't like to say no. Maybe he's just too nice to run production. He's lost control of the operation. I mean his people love him, but they don't produce. Quality problems. Cost overruns. Late deliveries. Chaos on the floor. It's a nightmare."

"Okay," said Vicky, taking notes. "You're seeing things we need to fix in product development and in manufacturing. Anything else?"

"Well, again, I hate to say this, Vicky," Madison said and then paused for emphasis. "Well, frankly, we could use some professionalism in our sales operation."

"How so?"

"Gene's an old-school salesman. Relies on chatting up the customers instead of product knowledge. And let me tell you, he's the master of the three-martini lunch. Sometimes more than three, I might add. His people follow the leader. Our products are getting more complex, but the sales force isn't keeping up. I have to constantly coach them, and hope there'll be adequate follow-up once an order is placed."

"Why's that?"

Madison looked down and sighed. "Well," she paused. "You've met Lin. I mean, she's the nicest gal around and so well-meaning. But how can she support the operation if she's too shy to talk to people about what the numbers show?"

"You'd like to see Lin speak up more?"

"I think you've got it all, Vicky," Madison replied with a sigh.

"Your perspectives on these areas are very helpful, Madison. Thank you." Vicky waited to see if Madison had anything else to say.

"Anything else I need to know?" Vicky asked warmly. "How about marketing? Are there things you'd like to improve there?"

A trace of a frown hinted that Madison didn't appreciate the questions. But it was replaced quickly by her usual big smile. "Of course, Vicky. I embrace continuous improvement, and I'm always looking for ways to make marketing better. But I think you'll find that we're highly respected by our marketing peers. Frankly, some of my colleagues here don't know enough about marketing to recognize the quality of what I do, but I think we compare very well to anyone in our industry."

Vicky left the meeting with Madison mulling a mix of feelings. Madison's candor was helpful in identifying issues that needed further investigation. But Vicky worried that this might be the first of a series of meetings in which people blamed everyone but themselves. And Vicky had a suspicion that despite her protests, Madison wasn't at all reluctant to criticize her colleagues.

8

Data

THE WOODEN DESKTOP WAS EMPTY except for a neatly stacked pile of folders in a simple wire basket on the right side, two pens and a mechanical pencil in a small ceramic tray in the center, and a black stapler on the left parallel to the telephone. The computer on a side table was showing multiple spreadsheets.

Lin is a classic clean desk manager. I hope that's a good sign, Vicky thought as she entered Lin's office. She was mindful of Madison's concerns about Lin, but eager to get to know Lin better. *Lin is key to understanding our operations in Dallas,* Vicky thought. *I need to get her talking.*

"Good morning, Lin. May I sit down?"

Lin looked up at Vicky, nodded, and then looked down. Vicky took the seat in front of Lin's desk.

"As business officer, Lin, I hope you can help me make sense of all that's been happening. I'm sure you're aware that the group's results have been disappointing, and it's our job to fix that. Where do you suggest we start?"

Lin nodded and reached for the folders in the in-basket. She put the stack in front of her, took the file on the top, and placed it open on her desk in a way that Vicky could read it.

"This might help," Lin began in a voice barely above a whisper. "Summary charts of our operations over the last five years. I can answer any questions. Our full financials to date are also in this folder."

"Great! This is great," Vicky said, happily pleased by Lin's initiative and preparation for the meeting. "Seeing the numbers over time is really going to help me understand where we've been. Very helpful. What else do you have for me?"

Lin took the second folder from the stack, turned it around, and again placed it open in front of Vicky to read.

"Some figures on our production operation. The charts show escalating cost overruns and steady increases in returned merchandise over the past six quarters."

Vicky looked down at the open file. Before she could comment, Lin pushed the rest of the stack across the desk.

"Please notice in these the following. The next folder details rising expenses over the last three years for the disposal of scrap metals and hazardous waste. Our scrap this fiscal year is 13 percent higher than industry standard and 2 percent higher than last year. The remaining two folders contain sales figures from the past five years for each product line with comparisons to our two major competitors. You'll see we're falling behind in new products to market."

Lin looked up briefly, met Vicky's eyes, and then looked down in her usual style. Vicky thought she saw a slight smile.

"Lin, this is very helpful. I'll study it all, and may be back to you with questions. I'm curious, who's seen this data?"

"I've always sent these reports to my boss. I gave these to Ted when he was here and to Barry before him. After that, I'm not sure."

"Well, that's something we need to change. I want everyone on the team to see the numbers. I'll be asking you to help on that, Lin," Vicky added. Lin shook her head yes, and again Vicky saw her slight smile. "Anything else I should know?"

"I'll send you a copy of the spreadsheets electronically. You'll find everything is accurate," said Lin. "I always double-check my work."

"I don't doubt that." Vicky smiled, stood up, and took the stack of folders from the desk. "I'll be back to you with any questions. Thanks, Lin. This is very helpful."

"Okay. Bye."

9

Underperforming

HOURS OF PORING OVER LIN'S data made it clear to Vicky that her meeting with Carlos had to be a candid talk about production. When she arrived in his office, he greeted her warmly and with a big smile.

"Vicky," Carlos said with an outstretched hand. "I've been waiting to show you the heart and soul of this unit. How about some coffee first?"

"Sounds good."

"I always keep a fresh pot. It encourages people to stop in. Great way to build rapport and learn about what's happening."

Vicky thanked Carlos and took a sip. She was encouraged by his warm welcome and glad that he encourages visitors.

"Hmm, Carlos. This is really good for office coffee!"

"It's a Guatemalan medium roast." Carlos smiled in appreciation of the compliment. "Another reason you shouldn't be a stranger down here, Vicky. It's a motivator to everyone when the big boss pays a visit. Hasn't happened in a long while. So, where should we start? Talk first, then tour or vice versa?"

"I'm looking forward to a tour, Carlos. Let's talk first so that I understand what I'm seeing."

"Sounds good." Carlos motioned toward the two comfortable chairs near the coffee pot. "Let's sit here. No desk to get between us. I like that in my meetings. And you'll be close enough for a refill when you're ready."

Vicky smiled. She felt more like herself in anticipation of this discussion — relaxed and ready to get down to the work at hand — than at any time since her arrival in Dallas. *Ironic,* she thought. *This could be one of the toughest conversations I need to have.*

"Carlos," she began. "I'm sure you're aware that the group's results have been disappointing and that it's our job to fix that. Let's begin with your sense of what's working well in your area and where things need attention."

"Since I've come on as head of production, we've made a lot of progress. Morale was very bad when I arrived, and we've got a real sense of family now. People enjoy coming to work and working here, Vicky, and that's important."

"Very true. And what about progress in your production numbers and your financials?

Carlos hesitated for a minute and then began. His smile was more forced. "We're a committed workforce. My gang will do whatever it takes, and I know we can do better. I just didn't have that before."

"That's important progress, Carlos," Vicky said with sincere appreciation, and she took a moment to let that sink in.

"It's good that you see that," Carlos said.

"Carlos, right now I need your help understanding some of the statistics I've seen recently. How do you make sense of the cost overruns? Missed delivery targets? And we seem to have quality problems. Too much returned merchandise. What's happening there?"

"Well, wow," Carlos stuttered. "Tell me, Vicky, what figures are you looking at? It'll be easier for me to be helpful if I know more specifically what you're referring to."

"Sure," Vicky responded, wondering why Carlos would be asking a newcomer about data on his operation. "Let me send you the stats that I've been studying and some additional data on our expenses for scrap and hazardous waste disposal. Have you been getting this kind of information?"

Carlos shook his head no. The smile was now completely gone from his face.

"Let's plan to meet again once you've seen the data, and we'll go over the reports," Vicky proposed. "I need you to help me understand what those figures mean."

"Absolutely. I'll study them all and have the answers for you in a week or so."

"Let's try for the day after tomorrow, Carlos. Can you check your calendar now for when you're free? We'll want a full hour."

"Absolutely. And maybe we should postpone the tour until then, too, Vicky," Carlos said. "It'll give me more time to prepare for our next meeting. I want to help."

10

The Check-in

A PACKED MORNING. MEETINGS. The usual flood of e-mail. Phone ringing. Calls from Carlos seeking reassurance—or forgiveness. Self-promotional updates from Madison. Assorted grumbles from Nathan. Rambling messages from Gene. All punctuated by periodic growls and edicts from Michael—by e-mail, phone, or in person—about fixing things and fixing them fast.

Vicky frowned as the phone rang yet again until she read the caller ID. Then she smiled broadly.

"Peter," she said, skipping the hello. "Some good news. I'm beginning to make headway."

"Sounds great."

"Like peeling an onion. One layer after another."

"Peeling onions can make you cry, Vicky."

"True, but it's worth a few tears if you like the results."

"So, what's cooking?"

"Well, when Michael said 'motley crew,' he wasn't exaggerating."

"No surprise."

"Any one of these people would be a challenge. I've got a whole team! Each difficult in a different way."

"So what'd you get dealt?"

"Oh," laughed Vicky. "Not the full house I would have liked."

44

"Any high cards?"

"I've got a business officer who's really on top of things. She helped me see a lot quickly. Had a stack of documents ready that I wouldn't have even known to ask for."

"Sounds like a keeper."

"Yes," Vicky said, then quickly added, "Well . . ."

"You're not sure?"

"Lin's smart and works like a beaver. But she could have been in silent movies. Shyer than a church mouse, as the saying goes. Doesn't look you in the eyes. And she never speaks up."

"Is she giving you what you need?"

"So far. But how can she support the operation if she's too shy to talk to people about what the numbers show?" Vicky was surprised to hear herself repeating Madison's question.

"Need a big talker or a good numbers cruncher? Anything off in what she gave you?"

"No. Just the opposite. She answered questions I didn't know to ask."

"Hmm . . ." Peter drew out the syllable and paused. In the silence, Vicky found herself wondering, *so why am I uncomfortable around Lin?* She scribbled herself a quick note to think further on that.

Peter brought her back to the conversation. "Okay. What about the rest?"

"There's Nathan. He heads R and D. A smart engineer and a world-class curmudgeon. He's so slow our competitors are running right over us."

"Any sense why?"

"He's an engineer, Peter," Vicky said, and they both laughed. "He likes to tinker, think, and make things. He's meticulous and careful, and proud of it. Doesn't like to be bothered and can't figure out why people don't just leave him alone."

"So you're late to market?"

"We're late on everything, but it's not just Nathan. There's Carlos in production. The nicest guy in the world, and his crew would do anything for him. But he's lost, and so is his operation."

"Okay. Who else?"

"Gene. Maybe one of the best sales managers of the last century, but it's not clear he can give us what we need now. He's hazy about our products, and he doesn't seem to notice or, worse yet, care. The rumor is he's a real drinker."

"Not good. How about marketing?"

"Madison."

"Great name for a marketer."

"And she's good in a lot of ways. Great presence. Articulate. Confident. But maybe even better at promoting herself and throwing others overboard. I'm not sure how much of this mess she owns, and she's not helping me figure that out. Worse," Vicky admitted with some reluctance, "I'm not sure if I can trust her. That's the crew."

"You've done good detective work. Now the question is what to do with it all. Have you got your *problem people plan* outlined yet?"

"Not yet," Vicky said with a deep sigh. She was suddenly beginning to feel just how tired she really was. Peter took note of the sigh, and said nothing about it.

"Important, Vicky. You'll burn out fast if you don't have a clear plan to help you cut through the confusion."

"I know. This isn't the first time you've given me that advice."

"In the middle of the fray it's easy to get caught up fighting each new fire, and forget that the plan's the thing."

"You're right. So how about a quick review of Peter's principles for a problem people plan for someone feeling rather exhausted at the moment?"

"*Sure*," he answered, drawing the word out. Vicky laughed. She knew he meant SURE, the acronym for the *four rules of engagement* for handling difficult people problems at work.

"Let's start with where you are."

"Well, I'm *sure* working hard," Vicky answered with a lilt. She knew Peter would enjoy that, and it felt good to bring some levity to the situation. "Trying to get the big picture. Making sure I'm looking at the full situation and not just individuals. Not jumping to conclusions."

"That's good."

"I've been meeting with people. Making notes. Thinking about myself and how I'm responding to what's in front of me. Looking for patterns. Trying to stay open to possibilities. Learning a lot."

"Good start. Stop, look, and learn." Peter heard Vicky sigh again. "You cutting yourself some slack here? This is a marathon, you know, not a sprint."

"Trying to." Vickie groaned softly. "But I feel people pushing my buttons at every turn. Michael with his putdowns and demands. And Madison's self-promotion is getting old already. Unhooking is east to say, hard to do."

"You're trapped unless you can unhook."

"I know! I know! And I feel more myself when I do it. Better able to get perspective. Like I'm up on the balcony and able to see the action on the whole dance floor below"

"So you see the full picture, not just the whirl around you."

"And, I feel more hopeful about sorting through the mess. Able to try some new things—especially with Michael. I think I'm starting to head in the right direction."

"What are you doing with Michael?"

"Stop, look, and learn is working for me. I'm studying him and my reactions to him. Unhook. He provokes me one way or another every time we meet, but I'm taking the time I need to get ahold of my feelings so I can stay on task. Revise the script. My new script is proactive positivity. I'm trying to kill him with optimism and good cheer. And the essence of the positivity strategy is engagement— move toward him rather than reacting to his latest attack."

"Sounds like you're ready to start drafting that plan."

"Oh, I already have directions in mind," Vicky said quickly and confidently. "I've met individually with each of the team, and I'm about to make another round. Clarify what they need to do their jobs better. Make it clear that I know what they're up against and that I want them to succeed."

"Sounds like Step 1 of Peter's principles for a problem people plan to me. It'll tell you pretty quickly whether the problem is individual performance or something more systemic. Any more?"

"Sets me right up for Step 2. Find ways to encourage people to learn and grow."

"Sounds like you know what you need to work on."

"Let's hope it works. Otherwise, it may be time for some fare-wells." Vicky took a deep breath. "But I hope it doesn't come to that."

"I hope not, too. But be ready to face it if you have to."

Vicky frowned. "Firing someone is never easy."

"No, but sometimes it's the best thing you can do. Take a shot at your plan," Peter added, "then give me a call. Choreograph how you want to lead the dance, Vicky, and see how they follow. Let's hope you'll be dancing with stars."

Interlude 3

Learning with Tenacity

VICKY APPROACHES THE NEW JOB IN DALLAS with the skills of a good detective and the calm persistence of someone who enjoys puzzles. Both serve her well. Starting a new job is difficult under the best of circumstances. A turnaround assignment with an underperforming team and a bullying boss could easily become a train wreck. Anyone in Vicky's shoes might feel tempted to grab at quick fixes or succumb to doubts about the wisdom of taking on Dallas. But Vicky stays focused and open: determined to get a full and accurate picture of what she is up against. She surfaces new information and different concerns in each meeting and demonstrates patience and a dogged focus on learning about her coworkers, herself, and the situation.

Vicky's approach provides an instructive example of using the SURE model. In the early going, she tenaciously embraces learning and puts particular emphasis on the first two *rules of engagement,* using insights gained from them to inform her choices in the other two.

1. **Stop, Look, and Learn: Questions, Answers, More Questions**
   In her early days in Dallas, Vicky focuses on studying the system and the individuals, probing how others see themselves, each other, and the situation. In talking to Michael and

members of her team, she hears conflicting stories about what's wrong, what needs to be fixed, and what she should do. She works at making sense of all this and avoids quick judgments about who or what is right. She tests her assumptions and evolving assessments with individuals, asking questions, and gauging their reactions.

Vicky is surprised to learn in her meeting with Carlos, for example, that he is hazy about the data on his operation. She comes away with specific questions to test and discuss at their next meeting. Does Carlos have the training and support to do the job? Is he getting the information he needs and in a timely fashion? Does he know how to understand and use it? Exploring these issues enables Vicky to clarify the present and plan for moving ahead. It also gives her opportunities to give Carlos feedback on his current performance, assess his openness to learning, and coach him toward where he needs to be. Diagnosing situations is like good detective work: an iterative process of collecting information, figuring out what it tells you (and doesn't), and testing hunches about what's happening and what more you need to know.

Vicky appreciates that organizations are complex systems, and assembles all the information she can: Lin's analyses, Michael's personnel files, notes from team meetings, individual interviews with each member of the team, and more. She also records her observations, feelings, and reactions at each turn— a way to check her memory and keep track of the action. Vicky uses a process of systematically collecting data, interpreting it, and taking action, recognizing that she'll learn more as she goes along. Good sense-making is at the heart of good leadership[1]—and vital in a messy situation like Dallas.

Vicky notices, for example, that Carlos is positive, enthusiastic, and beloved by his subordinates. She enjoys her interactions with him, and he seems open to working closely with her and others. That leaves the question of why the dismal operational results. Madison gives her a clue when she describes Carlos as having come up through the ranks and "in over his head." That points to possible learning gaps for Carlos and questions Vicky can explore to test his abilities and potential.

Branding others as difficult is a tempting way to simplify, but jumping to conclusions can block you from finding ways to stop bad behavior and encourage more productive contributions. A key test of a genuinely difficult person is whether the problematic behavior is rigid and uninfluenceable. Does the individual learn or adapt in response to feedback or clear expectations? Was there a particular incident or set of circumstances that triggered the behavior pattern? Does the individual's behavior vary with different people or circumstances? Indications that the behavior can be altered offer hope for a win-win,[2] and Vicky begins to see hope for Carlos.

Vicky also understands the importance of looking in the mirror to separate what's her from what's not. When others seem unreasonable, uncooperative, or ineffective, it's important to remember that they may see you as the problem—and they may be right. There may be feedback that you are not hearing or things you are doing that elicit unhelpful responses from others. You may be overresponding to behaviors that you alone see as troublesome or that trigger some unresolved life issues for you. If so, changing how you behave may quickly alleviate the problems you see in others.

2. **Unhook: A Mentor Helps**

Vicky is fortunate to have Peter as a guide and ally. Going it alone makes it hard to escape emotional turmoil and get the distance and perspective you need to understand your contribution to the situation—or to get the support to endure grueling circumstances. If you don't have a ready mentor like Peter, look for someone you can consult: a current or former boss, trusted colleague, professional coach, former teacher, or good friend. Wanting to learn and looking for help are signs of strong professionalism, not weakness. They are also vital for managing complex situations like those Vicky found in Dallas—and for staying both grounded and sane as you do. People who think and act in ways we wish they didn't often fall into our lives. There is no easy escape or quick fix. The central question is how to respond. Vicky offers a model of self-reflection and empowered engagement as she applies the SURE principles and deepens her understanding of herself and her circumstances

3. **Revise the Script: Calm, Assertive Leadership**

Vicky has inherited an underperforming, chaotic operation and knows she has to orchestrate a change in the script. She begins by writing a new one for herself that breaks historical patterns in the Dallas office. Instead of mirroring Michael's top-down, badger-and-blame leadership, Vicky approaches her team with an emphasis on learning, open communication, valid information, and teamwork.

In her initial meetings with members of her team, Vicky uses a combination of personal warmth, clarity of purpose, and a strong desire to learn. She compliments Madison for her office décor and Carlos for his coffee, and asks both of them tough questions. She discovers a number of recurrent patterns—old scripts that individuals continued to follow despite poor results. No one sets out to fail, but people often persist in following unproductive scripts when they lack clear feedback to help them see the need for change or they don't have the knowledge, skills, or confidence to do something different. Lin, for example, is superb at collecting and analyzing data, and weak at getting anyone to pay attention to her work. Vicky suggests sharing Lin's data with the entire team, and Lin's smile indicates her pleasure at being encouraged to assume a more proactive role. Carlos uses his geniality and interpersonal skills to mask his managerial and technical deficiencies. Vicky interrupts his script by arranging for him to get the data he needs and insisting that he review the numbers with her—sooner, rather than later. Vicky's calm yet assertive leadership pulls team members into the search for answers, and helps them see ways to play their roles more effectively.

4. **Engage: Build Relationships of Shared Accountability**

Vicky has entered an office culture of defensiveness, competition, mistrust, and mutual blame. Everyone knows the unit is failing and blames someone else. No one feels personally responsible for the problems or a solution, and the revolving door of people in Vicky's position suggests that her predecessors have been axed for failing to perform a nearly impossible job. Instead of pouring more blame and criticism into the mix, Vicky's actions convey that she expects everyone to be part of the solution. She approaches each individual with a message of, "Help me learn how we can work better together." She meets team members in their own offices—a small but important symbolic gesture, as Carlos notes when he tells her it has been a long time since a boss visited. Vicky asks open-ended questions such as, "Where should we begin?" before zeroing in with more specific and pointed ones like, "Are there things you'd like to improve?" She listens and checks to make sure she understands what people are telling her. She offers support, but leaves no doubt that she expects people will do their jobs and do them well.

Vicky certainly has challenges ahead and more to learn. So far, she is investing most of her time and energy in scouting and conveying that a new day is dawning. Peter reminds her that it's time to sketch out her game plan. It's tempting to want to know where every skeleton and bomb is buried, but it's a false hope that can keep you stuck. Information is always incomplete, but Vicky is getting clearer about where to begin. She needs to keep going. The plan can help her avoid the risk of fighting fires as they erupt around her, using precious resources—including time and social capital—on actions that may do little to address the root causes of her problems. Once Vicky has her game plan in place, she still needs to execute it. But she is building relationships and credibility with her team and laying a strong foundation for the work to come. Those are vital assets as she moves ahead.

PART IV

The Plot Thickens

11

Clarity

VICKY SAT AT HER DESK, puzzling over all she was learning. *So how much of what I'm seeing—Nathan's negativity, Gene's haziness, Carlos's cluelessness, Lin's reticence, Madison's slickness—is them, and how much is situational? Fuzzy expectations. Weak accountability. Training gaps. Strategy vacuum. A revolving door of bosses. I'll dig us all in deeper if I try to fix things before I know what the real problems are.* She began to write notes on the tablet in front of her.

Suddenly, Vicky stopped writing. She felt herself getting tense and took a moment to think about what that meant. She took a deep breath.

On one hand, I want to be fair to everyone, she thought. *I don't want to fire folks for the wrong reason. Do I have the wrong players? Or a workplace that's bringing out the worst in folks? If I just blame my motley crew, I might miss opportunities to ratchet up performance.* She jotted down a few more notes for herself.

On the other hand, Vicky admitted, *if I don't solve the people issues, the business and I are both sunk. The department will grind to a halt if I fire everyone, but I'm no magician. Even if I can bring out the best in each of them, will that be enough?* She was feeling more sympathy for her predecessors and more determined than ever to avoid their fate. Her renewed resolve buoyed her.

I know how to shape up rules and roles, she affirmed. *Distinguish between structural glitches and personalities. That's my starting point. It's always easier and cheaper to strengthen the team you have than to fire everyone and have to hire and train a host of new people.* She turned to the files spread across her desk.

Always start with what you know, she thought—and she could almost hear Peter's voice. *So what do I have?* She reviewed the folders. Lin's numbers. The personnel files Michael gave her. The things people said about one another. Her observations from watching folks in meetings. The early materials she got about Dallas. *I have more than enough to develop a preliminary picture*, she thought to herself. *Then I can get back with each individual, fill in the gaps, test my perceptions, and talk about the future. Job descriptions. Performance goals. Training needs.*Vicky liked the direction of her evolving plan.

And coaching folks through Step 1 could be fun, Vicky thought with a smile. *It'll give me a chance to get to know everyone better—and them, me. Have honest conversations. Clarify expectations. See how they respond. Let's hope most of them can step up to the plate! If not. . . .* Vicky stopped herself. *Well, I'll cross that bridge when I get to it.*

Peter's closing words in their last conversation echoed. How would she lead the dance? *He's right,* Vicky thought. She smiled as she thought: *maybe it's time for the waltz queen to learn to tango.*

12

Checking It Twice

IT HELPED VICKY TO SEE that she had options and a direction. She spent the rest of the day working on the details of her difficult people plan. She called Peter first thing the next morning.

"Are you ready to hear my plan?" she asked.

"I'm ready. Go for it."

"I've got to figure how to bring out the best in each of them."

"You hoping to save them all?"

"Ideally, yes. I don't know yet if I can. But I want to give everyone a chance."

"So where are you going to start?"

"Already did. Been sorting out how much is the individuals and how much is the chaos they've been living in.

"And?"

"I answered some nagging questions about operations. Carlos was thrown in at the deep end before he got a swimming lesson. With some training, he may be up to the job."

"Sounds good. So where you going next?"

"I keep thinking of Lin. She has great knowledge of the business, and she does a pretty good job of hiding it. I wish she were easier to talk with, more assertive, more of a leader."

"More like you?"

"I guess," Vicky said slowly as she thought about the truth in Peter's question. "I just don't like feeling that I have to drag stuff out of her. And I really need her to share her knowledge with the team. She won't do it unless she's asked."

"So why not ask her?"

Peter's question stopped Vicky. Then it hit her. "Of course. Yes."

The silence at the other end of the line told her to keep going.

"Sure. I could talk with her one-on-one before meetings. Tell her what I need from her and that I'll call on her for it. Coach her in advance so she's ready to answer. Then invite her in when I need her input."

"Think she can do it?"

"Actually, yes."

"It's not always easy, but I find I get better results when I move toward, not away from, folks whose styles really challenge me. Let's you see what's really there. You and Lin may find a way to work together where you both feel more comfortable."

"Move toward. Yes. Good reminder."

"My gift to you. Next?"

"Finding a better way to relate to Nathan. He really gets to me for some reason. In our one-on-ones, I try to stay calm. But his cranky, no-way-nothing-different attitude is tough to take. So negative. No enthusiasm. I've never been able to handle that stuff well."

"Hardest people to deal with are the ones who push our buttons. Know thyself."

"Sounds like another lecture on the benefits of unhooking coming," Vicky joked.

"I don't think you need it. You already know it's one of the hardest parts of a leader's job."

Vicky found herself needing to go on about Nathan. "The question is how. He brings out the worst in me."

"That's what makes difficult people difficult. You don't like what they're doing, but you get tied up in knots and you're at your worst when you need to be at your best."

"That I get, but what do I do about it?"

"How would you respond to Nathan if you were at your best?"

"I'd try to calmly talk to him about my concerns—our slow-to-market rate, how he thinks we can turn that around."

"What keeps you from doing that?"

Vicky thought about Peter's question before answering. "If I'm honest with myself, I just don't want him growling at me."

"How is that different from what you're facing with Michael?"

"Not very."

"And what do you do with Michael?"

"Avoid head-on collisions. Try to ask good questions. Remember he needs me as much as I need him."

"And would that work with Nathan?"

"It's worth a try. And I need to set clear expectations. Make sure he understands them. No big surprise that he's gone off track when no one's told him what he needs to do or holds him accountable for doing it."

"Your difficult people plan is coming together. You need to be proud of that," Peter said. "But, Vicky . . ."

"Yes?"

"Remember, don't invest in lost causes. You have to know when to hold. And when to fold."

"I'm working on that. And Peter . . ."

"Yes?"

"Thanks."

They ended their call, and Vicky got right to work. She set up meetings with each of her people. The way calendars lined up, it turned out that Carlos was up first.

13

Production

"READY FOR THE TOUR?" Carlos sounded upbeat, but he looked nervous.

"Sure," Vicky replied. "Lead on."

"You'll start with some coffee?"

"How can I pass up the best brew in the building?"

Vicky was eager to see the production operation and meet the staff. She was even more eager to check her take on Carlos. *Why is his operation out of control? Could he turn it around? Let's hope so,* Vicky thought. The thought of firing Carlos was almost too dreadful to contemplate.

The production floor looked familiar—high ceilings, fluorescent lights, dozens of workstations. Everyone looked to be hard at work, but Vicky sensed a frantic quality.

They were accosted almost immediately by a smiling, squat blond woman.

"Who's our guest today, Carlos?" she asked cheerfully. "Is this Vicky?" Without waiting for a reply, she introduced herself. "I'm Nina. Quality manager. It's great to meet you."

"I'm pleased to meet you, Nina. I'd love to learn more about our quality program."

"Anything you want to know. We're making progress. Maybe slower than we hoped, but we keep trying. Not there yet."

"Nina's doing a great job since she took over quality," Carlos interjected. "And she's only been in the job for less than a year."

"Tell me, Nina, what were you doing before you became our quality manager?"

"I was a shift supervisor here."

"She was our best, Vicky. Nina and I are both up from the ranks," Carlos added.

"I'm curious," Vicky asked, "Have you done anything with Six Sigma? ISO 9001?"

Nina and Carlos looked at one another. Neither looked comfortable.

"Well," Carlos stammered after a pause, "we've looked at that stuff. But we're so busy trying to keep the flow going, we haven't had time to figure out if any of it would help. That ISO stuff is real complicated. Lots of forms. We're kind of common sense on the floor. You know, just get it done."

"I'd better get back to work. Great to meet you, Vicky." Nina peeled off down an aisle of workstations.

"Carlos," Vicky said, trying to sound as positive as she could. "I think I can help. First, I'd like to bring in a consultant to work with you, take a look at the operations, make recommendations."

"Will Michael buy it?"

"Why not?"

"Well, about a year ago I asked Ted about getting a consultant. And some training for my people. He said he needed to check with Michael. It never happened."

"I'll clear it with Michael. Carlos, I'm impressed by a lot of what I'm seeing. Your relationship with your people. There's a real esprit de corps."

"Thanks, Vicky. We used to have a lot of labor strife, so I'm proud of what we've been able to do."

"That I see. But you've seen the numbers. We've got to improve our costs and quality."

"You have to understand, we're all working very hard on that."

"To be honest, Carlos, I think you're doing a great job on what you know how to do—build a great sense of family, workforce loyalty. I know you're working hard and doing the best you can. But we have to get you the help you need to turn this into a first-class production operation."

Vicky saw the pain in his face. She waited for him to respond.

"I know that, Vicky. I've known it for a long time. But, it's been pretty chaotic and not the most supportive in recent years. I never felt it was safe to admit that I didn't know something."

"We have to change that, Carlos. Going forward, we need to meet every week. Review your results. Talk about how we can work together and make this operation better."

"Sounds good. Very good," Carlos said, breathing a sign of relief. "And before you go, Vicky, let me get you a fresh cup of coffee."

Vicky left feeling more optimistic than when she arrived. *Carlos is smart, and the good news is that he knows he needs help,* she told herself. *If we can give him the training and technical tools he needs and hold his hand for a while, I think he'll make it. I sincerely hope so, anyway.*

Interlude 4

Leading with Purpose

FINDING A WAY OUT OF HELL IS often a defining moment for organizational leaders—a "crucible experience" in the words of leadership guru Warren Bennis.[1] Success requires the ability to persist when the going gets rough and to offer others an effective path forward. Successful leaders find ways to learn from negative events and help others do the same. As a result, they—and their organizations— emerge stronger and wiser, confirming to themselves and those around them that they have the right stuff for extraordinary impact.

In *The Prince*,[2] Machiavelli notes that crisis reduces resistance and opens the possibility of deep change. Vicky's challenge is finding the right course while in the middle of the storm. Her skill at using the four *rules of engagement* suggests that her operation can emerge as a very different and stronger workplace. When leaders learn, organizations often do as well.

1. **Stop, Look, and Learn: Study People in Context**
   Vicky wisely works to separate the people from the situation. Ineffectiveness that looks at first glance like a product of individual flaws is often rooted in situational pressures. When that is the case, changing the players may change nothing. Organizational roles, rules, and structures influence individual

actions, sometimes in ways the actors themselves don't see.[3] In cases like these, leaders need to understand and repair structural features like rules, procedures, and job descriptions.

It is tempting, for example, to blame Carlos for the quality and expense problems in his operation. After all, he is the manager in charge. But if the organization has failed to provide what he needs to do his job effectively, that problem needs to be solved first. Vicky sees that Carlos is doing well on what he knows how to do. Morale is up, and he has developed a loyal workforce. She also realizes that past bosses have not consistently shared Lin's data with him, nor have they confirmed that he knew how to interpret and use the information he had. Carlos and his quality manager, Nina, both came up through the ranks, and Carlos admits that he is inexperienced in various quality programs and systems. As happens too often, Carlos was promoted and then left to sink or swim on his own.

Vicky knows better than to start by blaming people. That's the simplistic way that managers often diagnose any problem.[4] Pinpointing a culprit is comforting and quick. But it can block you from seeing situational factors that may be more important, and it leaves you with fewer workable options. Carlos responds well to Vicky's offer that they meet and work more closely together. He trusts her enough to ask for help and admit his fear of acknowledging weakness. After careful study, Vicky concludes that giving Carlos coaching, training, and better data may lead to the improvement she needs. Going forward, she'll keep an eye on his progress to gauge whether that optimism is justified.

Good situational assessment is also informed by a respect for diversity in its many forms. A good example is Lin, whose reserved style may lend itself to what Lin likes doing—solo numbers crunching. Peter helps Vicky see that her problem with Lin is as much about Vicky's comfort as about Lin's competence in the basics of her job. We all enjoy working with people whose styles mesh well with our own. But comfort is a dangerous criterion for assessing performance and can purge an organization of vital differences that are the wellspring of innovation and change. The world grows increasingly diverse and with it the importance of distinguishing what is difficult from what is different.

Cultural differences, for example, may be at play between Lin and Vicky. Research on workplace behavior finds that employees with East Asian backgrounds, for example, are often (though not always) more deferent to the boss and less likely to initiate than their Western peers.[5] They can also exhibit communication patterns that differ from the jump-in, talk-over, rough-and-tumble speech patterns found in many Western cultures. Differences among national cultures are only one of many dimensions of diversity that play a significant role in the workplace. Gender, race, ethnicity, educational background, early life experiences, developmental perspectives, and other differences all influence how we perceive and relate to others at work.

If we look at Lin's behavior through a diversity lens, it takes on new meaning and confirms the value of Vicky's suggested coaching strategy. All the signs indicate that Lin is great with numbers and details, and wants to do a good job. Knowing that her boss wants her to share information with the team—and to initiate to get the data she needs to do that—sets clear expectations for Lin. Preparing Lin in advance for staff meetings encourages her to learn new behaviors. Even skilled and motivated people will be hard put to perform as needed unless they know what their job is and how their boss expects them to do it. Clarity of expectations makes it easier to intervene when someone goes off track. It also makes it easier to identify a genuinely difficult person.

Vicky's coaching goal to "bring out the best" in each individual has team implications, and team members will need Vicky's help learning new ways of seeing and working with one another. Lin may become more proactive with Vicky's help, and others will need to learn to respond positively to that and to Vicky's expectations that they will listen and take heed. Team dynamics can support or impede individual learning and development.

2. **Unhook: Cultivate Mental Strength and Strategies**

Peter confirms what Vicky is already feeling: unhooking is one of the hardest parts of a leader's job—and it is an ongoing task. She may grumble to Peter about Nathan and Michael pushing her buttons, but Vicky shows remarkable ability to stay grounded and task-focused. Four of her strategies are helpful to add to your repertoire of skills.

1. *Treat difficult people as you would others with whom you feel comfortable.* Difficult people evoke stress and discomfort that cause you to relate to them differently. You fear their behavior and how you feel in the face of it, and seek to avoid the distress. That launches a pattern of awkward avoidance. Think about how you would approach the same conversation if you were talking with a close friend or colleague. What would you say? How would you say it? Do the same with your difficult person.

2. *Ask questions.* We have noted that Vicky is a master of inquiry. It helps her learn, and conveys her sincere interest in others. Both are paths to a trusting relationship. Suspending judgment encourages increased candor. Building a relationship with difficult others makes them less scary and unpredictable.

3. *Listen actively.* It is a workplace staple that bosses claim to listen, yet never do anything about what they've been told. Vicky employs an iterative process of listening carefully, testing for understanding, and then closing the loop by responding to what she hears. Active listening has roots in the person-centered therapy and personal growth techniques pioneered by Carl Rogers more than 75 years ago, and is a proven way to boost problem solving capabilities. Your difficult person may be difficult because no one listens!

4. *Track what works.* Vicky notes after her first meeting with Michael that questions work with him. She plans to test if the same might be true with negative Nathan. These are examples of the value of keeping notes and reflecting on patterns.

Vicky seems blessed with mental strength, which psychologist Amy Morin describes as the ability to regulate your emotions, manage your thoughts, and behave in a positive manner despite the difficult situations and people you may face.[6] Everyone enjoys some degree of mental strength, and there's always room for more. Vicky makes good use of each talk with Peter to build hers.

Enhancing your mental strength requires a three-pronged approach: replacing irrational thoughts or fears with more realistic assessments, behaving in a positive manner when tempted otherwise, and controlling your emotions so they don't control you. It's not about acting tough, burying feelings, or emulating Pollyanna. Rather, it's about authenticity: knowing who you are, what you believe and value, and how to control your feelings and behavior for a productive response to whatever comes your way.

3. **Revise Scripts: See Progress, Find Joy**

   In her first round of meetings with Michael and her new team, Vicky relies on a script focused mostly on inquiry: asking questions and listening to get a read on the individuals and circumstances. Then she took time to review what she was learning, plan how to move forward, and check signals with Peter. She emerges with a new script that retains the elements of inquiry and listening, but adds gentle confrontation and setting new directions. Her meeting with Carlos is her first to use this new approach. In round one, she encourages others to lead and she tries to follow. Now Vicky is ready to take the lead herself.

   Both Vicky and Peter, however, notice signs of her growing fatigue. Burnout is inevitable in situations like hers without ways to sustain stamina and drive. Taking pleasure in small successes and finding joy in the middle of the storm both help: Vicky recognizing, for example, the fun in coaching Lin and others is a move in the right direction. Nourishing the soul and sustaining health and vitality are ongoing leadership challenges.[7] They are vital when navigating rough waters.

4. **Engage: Move Toward, Not Away**

   Peter reminds Vicky that it is counterintuitive but vital to reach out to those who confuse or trouble us. Moving toward difficult people—getting to know them better and trying to learn more about their needs, concerns, choices, and feelings—can go a long way toward improving a relationship. If individuals feel better understood, respected, and appreciated, they are better able to hear feedback and more willing to engage in fruitful discussion. Vicky won't find out if Lin, for example, can interact differently with her or with the team by pulling back from someone she finds "shyer than a church mouse." By moving closer, Vicky can encourage Lin to contribute in ways Vicky needs and identify strategies that fit for Lin. She also demonstrates a respect for Lin and confidence in her abilities to grow in the job. Continued dialogue may enable both women to discover new ways to work together.

Similarly, Vicky is put off by Madison's pattern of critiquing everyone but herself; it won't help for Vicky to pull back. She may lose a talented contributor, and Madison won't learn how to strengthen her team skills. Reaching out is also a good diagnostic device to see whether you are dealing with someone who can respond to clear feedback and rational dialogue, as opposed to a candidate for separation, counseling, or serious professional intervention.

Moving toward a difficult person doesn't mean false intimacy or colluding in inappropriate behavior. It is a process of showing genuine interest in another so as to understand him or her better. Managers who develop greater rapport with their coworkers have a better chance at influencing them. Even difficult people listen better to those who demonstrate an ethic of interest and concern.

PART V

Fix or Fold

14

Sales

GENE'S ASSISTANT SEEMED NERVOUS. "I'm sorry," she stammered. "I'm sure he knows about your meeting. But, um, but he's not back from lunch. Uh, you know, sometimes he gets held up."

"Lunch with a customer?" Vicky asked pleasantly.

"Um, well, yes. I'm sure it must be something like that."

"I understand," Vicky said. "Can you let me know when he's ready?"

"Oh, absolutely," the assistant promised.

I hope it's just the life of a salesman, Vicky thought to herself. But she feared worse—Gene's assistant seemed to be trying to cover for her boss. Was this a bad omen?

Gene was wearing a big smile when they met half an hour later in his office. "Couldn't get away from a customer," he said in a brief apology. But his face was flushed, and the smile seemed forced. Vicky sensed that something wasn't right.

"Who were you meeting with?" she asked.

"Old customers, you wouldn't know them." Vicky didn't appreciate the brush-off.

"With your help, I'll get to know a lot of our customers. But for now, I'd like to talk more about what the sales force can do to improve our business results."

"I hope you know how tough it is out there," Gene said.

"I'm sure it is, Gene, and I want to know about your challenges. I have some questions, and I hope you have ideas on how we can get better."

"You know how hard we've been working?" Gene's smile was gone, and he sounded angry and combative.

"Can you tell me about that?"

Gene hesitated, as if surprised by the question. "Well, I mean, hard. Really hard."

"Say more," coaxed Vicky. "I'd like to hear about what's been happening in sales." Gene just glared at her.

Vicky broke the silence. "We need hard work, Gene, but we need to make sure we're working on the right things. Tell me if I'm wrong, but when I look at our results, we seem to be skewed toward selling old products to the same old customers."

"Hell, in this economy, we're lucky to sell anything to any customers." Gene's expression had turned sour, but Vicky was more concerned that his speech seemed slurred. Had Madison been right when she hinted that Gene had a drinking problem?

"Sure, Gene," Vicky said pleasantly. "We want to keep our best customers. But it's tough to make money selling old products with weak margins."

"Tell me something I don't know." Gene's volume was increasing and his tone was even more combative.

"I'm sure you know it, Gene," Vicky said calmly, "but I'm interested in what you and the sales force can do to sell more of our new, higher-margin products."

"We try, but the new stuff is too expensive," he growled. "It's unproven. Our customers don't want it."

"Let's reconfirm our pricing, Gene. That's important," Vicky said, making a note. "And can you help me understand why the competition is doing better than we are in promoting new products?"

"When in the hell did you ever sell anything, lady? What makes you think you know the first thing about customers? Our customers?" Gene's face was bright red, and he was almost bellowing at Vicky.

Vicky had sensed that Gene might explode, but she was still startled. *Go slow,* she told herself. *Don't make this worse.*

"Gene," she said quietly, "let's meet again when you're fully ready for a business discussion."

"You're telling me I'm not ready? I am ready." He jumped up and pushed his chair back. He used his desk to steady himself as he leaned toward Vicky. He was shouting. "You're the one who's never sold anything in your life, but you think you can come in here and tell me how to do my job."

Vicky remembered one of Peter's rules. When other people get angry, don't escalate; inquire.

"Gene," she said, speaking softly. "Can you tell me what I said that implied that?"

Gene hesitated. Again he didn't seem to expect the question. "Oh, hell. Everything."

"It'll help if you can be more specific. Give it some thought, and let's plan to meet again. Is tomorrow morning good for you?"

Gene sat back down and stared. He looked deflated. Was he realizing that he had dug himself into a deep hole?

"I'll confirm with your assistant," Vicky said as she stood up. "See you tomorrow, Gene."

Once back at her office, she quickly texted Peter. "Met another dragon. Avoided flames. Town may not be big enough for both of us."

She wasn't surprised when Peter called a few minutes later.

"So, who was breathing fire on you this time?"

"My sales manager."

"What happened?"

"He was half an hour late for our meeting. Said he was with a customer, and I'm pretty sure he was drinking. When I asked him how we could improve our sales he started shouting at me that I'd never sold anything but was trying to tell him how to do his job."

"What did you say?"

"You'd have been proud. Followed your advice and asked him calmly what I'd said that suggested that."

"Staying cool under fire. Asking a good question. I'm proud. So, now what?"

"You always said divorce only if necessary. Well, I wish it weren't, but I'm thinking it may be. He probably didn't know what he was doing, but he basically volunteered to walk the plank. Gave me nothing to work with. Confirmed my worst fears. And if he'll yell at his boss, you wonder how he treats everyone else." Vicky took a deep breath and leaned back in her chair. "By the end of the meeting, I think he realized it. We're meeting tomorrow. I'll ask him if he sees a future here. Assuming he's sober, I think he'll go quietly. I can offer him severance, counseling, placement services—an offer I'm pretty sure he won't refuse."

"What's his track record been before this?"

"Lousy. And lousy for a long time."

"Okay. I don't like to give up on someone based on one meeting, but sounds like not a lot of reasons to keep your dragon. Sleep on it, and see if it still feels right in the morning. Good luck tomorrow."

15

A Warning from Michael

THINGS ARE COMING TOGETHER, Vicky thought as she sat at her desk. Plenty of problems, but she was feeling more confident that they could be fixed. She remembered the old leadership wisdom: when you understand, you know what to do.[1]

Vicky turned to her computer. She wanted to make some visuals to capture what she was seeing. She planned to share them with Michael. If understanding the big picture was helping her, she hoped the same would be true for him. She also knew it was important to keep him informed and involved in her turnaround strategy.

A loud rap on the door jamb gave her a start.

"Oh, Michael," Vicky said looking up. "Come in. Please." Seeing Michael at the door reminded her that he was still near the top of her difficult people list. Shoring herself up for every surprise and verbal assault was going to wear thin. She took a deep breath and smiled. "I think I'm starting to get a handle on things here."

Michael stood at the door. "You're out of touch. People say you're not leading. They don't like working with you. They're losing confidence." He turned and walked away.

Vicky wanted to scream. Or cry. Or chase after Michael to tell him he was the most destructive boss she'd ever known. She sat staring at her computer screen as a jumble of emotions swirled through her, taking plenty of deep breaths and then a distracting moment of pleasure looking at the flowers on her desk.

After the wave passed, Vicky tried to make sense of their encounter. *What is he up to? That was an ambush. Twisting the knife when I didn't expect it. But I shouldn't be surprised. Michael was just being Michael, and he's so good at it that it's almost impossible not to get hooked. But unhooking is exactly what I need to do. Letting my anger take over won't help me or anyone else.*

Vicky took another deep breath, then reached for the phone and dialed. Peter was in a meeting. She left word.

16

Hate Your Boss?

"IS IT OKAY TO HATE your boss?" Vicky asked.

"Maybe," Peter replied, "But not very helpful. What happened?"

"Drive-by assault. I was in my office, thinking about good news I could share with Michael. He pops in, tells me my group is losing confidence because I'm not leading. Then he disappears while my jaw is still dropping."

"That came out of the blue?"

"Totally. And I just lost it. It's good he got out quick, because otherwise I might have said something stupid. I understand why they say revenge is a dish best served cold." They both laughed. "But I'm feeling a little calmer now. Hey, thanks for calling me back so soon."

"So, what do you make of this?"

"Someone in my group has been talking to Michael, and probably getting rewarded for it. And Michael's so slick that he wants plausible deniability. He can say I asked for 'no surprises' and he was just trying to help me out with honest feedback."

"Why would someone be feeding Michael?"

"To stay on his good side. To make nice to the dragon." Vicky swallowed hard and continued. "Michael's like the abusive parent around here, Peter. Everyone sees how he'll turn on anyone in a flash. Blind-side you when you least expect it. Hold back what you

79

need to do your job and then blame you when you can't do it. Nobody wants to be the next target, so they try to stay on his good side. Curry favor with gossip and tidbits. Show him they're on his side."

Vicky paused to think about the full implications of what she was saying. Peter waited. Then she began again. "I think Michael has created a culture of fear around here where people tell him stories about one another all the time. You know, compete for his love, get him to go after somebody else so they stay out of his line of fire. It's one of the reasons this place is such a mess. And why this team, for as long as it's been together, is not a team."

"Any suspects?"

"More than one. Gene might have said something on his way out the door. And I'm not sure how far I can trust my marketing manager."

"So now what?"

"Well, eventually, I need to take on Michael. But first I need to make sure I've got my troops behind me."

"Question: is Michael completely unpredictable?"

"Completely?" Vicky mused. "You know, I think the answer is yes and no. What's really unpredictable is you never know when he'll show up or what exactly he's going to say. But whenever he appears, there's a good chance he'll be breathing some kind of fire."

"Then you need some kind of flame-proofing. For you. And for the team."

"Asbestos suits?"

"One option, I guess." Peter and Vicky both laughed. "I was thinking more about anticipating the plays you know Michael likes to run. If he's going to drop in and drop bombs, then expect it. Don't let it throw you. Figure out what you'll say and do when it happens. Don't give him the power of surprise. And, Vicky," Peter spoke softly now. "I wouldn't give up yet. Michael could be a nut that's too tough to crack. But I haven't seen too many of those. I've always given it my best for a while, and kept looking for a door to open somewhere that I just haven't found yet. Most times, it's there."

"I knew you wouldn't let me off the hook yet. I'll keep looking for that door."

"Let me know how things go. Okay?"

"I will. And I have one small request."

"Sure."

"If by chance you have a reason to call Michael in the next week or so, say something nice about me."

"My pleasure. That should be fun."

17

In Sheep's Clothing

I CAN COUNT ON MADISON *to be poised and prepared,* Vicky told herself. *I just hope I'm ready for her. I don't know for sure who's going behind my back to Michael, but Madison is a prime suspect.*

Once again, Madison was on her feet and smiling enthusiastically as she raced to the door to welcome Vicky into her office.

"Thanks for coming over, Vicky. I've been looking forward to our meeting. There's so much we can do, and I'd love to share my thoughts."

"Great. I'm eager to hear them, Madison."

"I should start by offering congratulations, should I not? Good work!"

Vicky was puzzled. "Which work?"

"Oh, I know it's not public yet, but I understand that we'll be hearing about a change in sales leadership before too long."

How, Vicky wondered, *did Madison know so much about something Gene and Vicky had discussed less than a day earlier?*

"The grapevine must be hard at work," Vicky replied.

"We'll tell everyone Gene is pursuing other opportunities, of course," said Madison amiably. "Actually, it should have happened sooner, but I don't blame you. I know some people who would be great candidates for Gene's job. I'll make sure they apply."

"Thanks," replied Vicky, even though "friend of Madison" was not at the top of her list of job qualifications. "We need really strong, experienced candidates. The job is so important."

"Absolutely," Madison agreed. "And this is a great opportunity to define the position in a way that improves coordination between sales and marketing."

"What are you thinking?"

"You know we've had problems getting the sales force aligned with our marketing direction. Sales was taking the easy way. Selling the old, low-margin stuff. We can solve that by having the new sales manager report to me."

Well, I'll be. Why didn't I see that coming? Vicky asked herself. She tried not to look surprised. "You think sales should report to you?"

"Oh, I know you're wondering why would I want to take on even more when I have so much to do. But, really, it'll make my job easier. I won't have to spend so much time trying to get the two groups on the same page."

Vicky wondered if Madison's next proposal would be to get perfect alignment by having everyone in the office report to marketing. "I agree with your goal," Vicky responded. "We do need to get sales and marketing working better together. Their shop and yours both need to have a strong voice in our business."

"That won't be a problem," Madison countered. "To be frank, I can advocate for sales better than Gene did."

"Have you worked in sales?"

"No, but I know what they need to do. And I've always been a quick study. I can pick up whatever I need."

"I admire your confidence, and we'd need to give that more thought. What other ideas do you have?"

"Well, that's number one. But we also have to do something about production. We can't build the business unless we can keep our promises to customers."

"I know we've had issues there," Vicky responded. "I'm working with Carlos, and I expect significant progress. At the same time, we need to emphasize teamwork—we're going to win or lose together, so we need to help one another succeed."

"A team can't win without the right players, Vicky. Why risk your career on someone who's blown it as much as Carlos has?"

Vicky wrestled with a mix of feelings. For as much as she admired confidence and directness, she wondered about Madison's ability to be a team player. *Well,* Vicky told herself, *listening and learning will only get you so far. It's time for some straight talk.*

"Madison, I value your honesty and initiative. You have a lot of ideas that we can use. But I sometimes get the message that you're okay, and everyone else is not. Your suggestions focus on fixing other people's operations. I'm learning from your input, but we need to strengthen everything we do, including marketing. What can we do to strengthen your area?"

Madison's face tightened, but she kept her veneer of perfect composure. "Well," she said, as the trace of a frown crossed her face, "if you don't want my suggestions. . . ."

"Madison, when did I say I didn't want your ideas?" Vicky asked with sincerity.

"Well, you're batting down everything I suggest."

"I do appreciate your insights, Madison. As well as your talent and willingness to speak up. That's why I'm here and why I want to get your ideas for making marketing even better. What would help you and your department do a better job?"

"That's exactly what I've been trying to explain. I need colleagues in this organization I can count on. And sales should report to me."

"I agree you need colleagues you can rely on. That's what teamwork is all about. We have to make sure you get the support you need, and we need a strong sales manager. Meanwhile, let's talk about marketing."

"You have nothing to worry about there."

"Great, then let's talk about your ideas going forward."

But Vicky never got what she was looking for. Madison was smooth and steadfast in depicting her operation as world-class and herself as the star player leading it. As Vicky became increasingly frustrated, she remembered Peter's advice: if all else fails, tell the truth.

"Madison," Vicky asked, "do you feel it's unreasonable for me to ask how marketing can improve its results?"

"Of course not," Madison replied.

"Here's what's worrying me, Madison. I don't hear anything about what you can do better. Instead, I hear that you need your teammates to pass you the ball so that you can score more."

Another frown flashed across Madison's face, but her smile was quickly back. "Vicky, it's not that I want to hog the ball. But, frankly, if they'll give it to me, I know what to do with it. They don't."

"Madison, this business is going to win or lose as a team. We need team players. I want you to have strong partners, and I want to be sure I can get the support I need from you. You need to decide if you really want to play on this team."

Madison's face flushed. For a moment, she was speechless. When she finally spoke, there was anger, albeit controlled, in her voice. "So, you're telling me it's your way or the highway!"

Vicky paused, looked Madison in the eyes, and spoke slowly and calmly. "Madison, not my way. The team's way. It's not about who gets top billing. It's about each area doing their best and working together to make our business successful. Give it some thought, Madison. Then let's meet again."

18

Fire Your Star?

"HAVE YOU EVER FIRED YOUR star player?"

Peter paused to think before answering, "Yes."

"Because you couldn't work with the person?"

"No. Because the evidence was clear the star made the team worse. It's the same in business or basketball. Talent without teamwork loses. But you've got to make sure your diagnosis is right. You don't want to create a problem by solving the wrong one. Who's your falling star?"

"Madison, my marketing manager."

"And?"

"When we met to talk about improving the business, her only ideas were to expand her empire and replace her colleagues."

"Could she be right?"

"Partly. She gave me critical information to understand Carlos, and she was right that our sales manager had to go. She even congratulated me for getting that done—but that's a story for another time. As I'm seeing it, our biggest problem is lack of coordination and teamwork."

"And she's not helping?"

"Only if she gets to be in the spotlight. Even a hint of criticism gets her pouting."

"When she pouts, what do you do?"

"At first, I was backing off. You know how well that works. When last time we met, I confronted her directly. Told her she needed to decide if she wants to sign up for the team."

"What did she say?"

"She took it as me telling her it was my way or the highway."

"Does she think the town isn't big enough for both of you?"

"Maybe. She talks as if she already has my job. Anyway, I told her that it's about making the team a success, not about who's the star. And I asked her to give that some thought."

"What do you expect she'll do?"

"Not sure. Best case is I got her attention. She's smart enough to realize it's good for both of us if we work together. Worst case is she prolongs the battle. Sees building the team as me holding her down. One thing I do know: Madison needs to help the team move forward or she has to go."

"Sounds like you did what you had to. You were clear, you gave her feedback, and you gave her a choice. In my experience, that works more often than not. Confront, offer a choice, and give some time to think. People often come around when they know what's expected of them."

"I hope so. I'd just as soon not lose her. Madison has a lot to offer."

"I hope not either. Firing is never fun."

"And to be fair," Vicky added, "Madison's's done a lot over the years to hold things together in the chaos."

"Hmm . . ." Peter mused, pausing before adding, "makes me wonder what Madison's losing in all this change."

Vicky hadn't thought about it that way and was glad for Peter's reminder to figure that out.

No sooner had Peter signed off than Vicky heard a tap on her door.

"Come in," she called.

Madison poked her head in. "Do you have a minute?" she asked.

"Of course, come on in."

"Vicky," Madison said, looking almost sheepish. "I've been thinking since our meeting. I've realized some things."

"I'd love to hear about them," Vicky responded warmly and motioned to the chair in front of her desk.

Madison hesitated, and then sat down. Vicky had never seen her so uncomfortable. "Well, I don't want to make excuses or dredge up my whole past." Madison paused and looked down, before continuing. "Well, when I was growing up, my parents were impossible to please. It always seemed that I was never as good as my beautiful and brilliant older sisters."

"It sounds painful," Vicky responded sincerely.

"It was." Madison hesitated. "Still is."

"So you've always had to fight for everything?"

"No one has given me anything. I know I sound like a whiney kid, but I feel I've worked so hard and never get the appreciation I think I've earned."

"You've felt that here as well?"

"Yes. Boss after boss didn't see what I was doing. Didn't thank me for taking on the extra work. And then they gave you the job I wanted."

"I wondered about that, Madison," Vicky replied gently.

Madison looked away and paused again. "To be honest, I probably underestimated you. I was expecting another weak boss. But you're smart and tougher than I thought at first. You know your stuff."

"Thanks, Madison. I think that's why I got the job."

"To be perfectly frank, that's another thing I realized. Someone up there in Corporate believes in you and what you can do." Madison paused. "This may sound awful, but I was figuring that you'd fail like the rest and then they'd finally give me the job to fix things up. When you told me either sign up for my job or look for a new one, I had to do some thinking. Where I come out is that right now the best thing I can do for my career is to help you succeed."

"And the best thing I can do for your career is to help you get set up for that promotion. That would be good for both of us," Vicky said with a smile.

Madison looked Vicky in the eyes, smiled slightly, and sounded more confident again. "I guess I'm saying, if you still want me on the team, coach, sign me up!"

"Of course I do! Working together, we can all win—and win big!"

As Madison left, Vicky knew that she was a work in progress. Madison's old wounds would not disappear overnight, and strengthening the team would mean a change in the kind of informal leadership

Madison had brought to it over the years. But Vicky also knew that Madison was a hard worker, had a good diagnostic sense, and showed a lot of courage in being so open and vulnerable. *Now,* Vicky thought, *I think we can work together.* Even more important, Madison now felt that she was better off joining Vicky than opposing her.

It'll take time and patience, Vicky thought, *and using Peter's advice to move closer. Time with Madison gives me opportunities for mentoring—and staying alert to any backsliding.*

Sun-tzu's famous quotation ran through Vicky's mind: keep your friends close and your enemies closer. Then she laughed as she remembered LBJ's coarser variation: it's always better to have someone inside the tent peeing out than outside the tent peeing in.

19

Back to the Boss

"WHAT IS IT NOW?" Michael grunted, as Vicky walked in after a soft rap on the door.

"Quick update. Part of the no surprises program."

"I don't suppose there's any good news."

"Actually, there is. After your feedback, I've been working on my leadership. And . . . I expect the numbers to come in above forecast."

"If they don't. . . ."

"I know—you'll have a public flogging. But it probably won't be necessary."

Michael looked at Vicky, his face frozen.

"So, here's the summary. We're going to give Carlos training, help, and the data he needs. I'll keep him on a short leash for a while, but he'll be fine. Madison has decided she wants to develop her teamwork skills, and I'm helping her on that. We got Nathan's attention with stats from Lin on how we stack up against our competitors, and he's working to make engineering faster and more flexible. He's getting help from one of his people who's got good management potential. Gene has resigned, so we need to find a replacement, and I'm ready to begin the search."

Michael continued staring at her. Vicky was pretty sure he was looking for something to criticize.

After a long pause, he said, "Sounds like fairy tales. You're just digging your own grave with that crew, but at least you figured out that Gene drinks more than he sells."

"Let's just say that after we talked, Gene decided he should seek other opportunities."

"Yeah, I'm sure of that. Oh, by the way, I got a call from Peter Frost at the head shop. He says he knows you."

"Peter? He was my first boss. He's been a great mentor."

"Yeah, so it seems," Michael said, sounding anything but pleased.

"Well, my approach is the same with you as it was with Peter. I try to make my boss look good. To be honest, one reason I have to make a go of this job is I'd hate to disappoint either of you."

"So don't."

"Even with your high standards, I don't plan to."

Vicky smiled as she left Michael's office. *He's trying to sound as tough as ever,* she thought to herself, *but maybe proactive positivity is starting to melt the iceberg. And Peter's call didn't hurt.*

Interlude 5

Move On? Push Out?

THE BASIC SURE PRINCIPLE IS SIMPLE. Engage first. Exit only if necessary. But how do you know when it's necessary? That question vexes Vicky. On the one hand, she wonders if she should fire members of the team she has inherited. On the other, she puzzles over how her relationship with Michael can ever work. If things aren't working, sometimes you have to move on—or push someone out. If you've persisted and done your best, and there are no signs a situation can be salvaged, it's time to face a hard and painful reality.

Consistent use of the SURE model should reduce the odds that you have to face the painful decision to fire someone or to exit from a relationship that can't be saved. Your difficult people may not become perfect, but things will usually improve enough that you can work together productively and strengthen that over time. But, in other cases, persistent application of the SURE principles may bring a different clarity: recognition that divorce is the best option. If you've persisted and done your best and there are no signs a situation can be salvaged, it may be time to face a hard and painful reality.

1. **Stop, Look, and Learn: Review and Reconfirm**

    In dealing with both her boss and subordinates, Vicky shows remarkable ability to take a long view. In stressful moments, she avoids acting on impulse or throwing in the towel at a first failure. Instead, Vicky takes time to reflect and, often, get input. She could have fired Carlos, Lin, or Madison; but in each case she studies the situation over time, concludes that optimism is justified, and looks for specific ways to remedy performance gaps. She knows what she expects from each, communicates that clearly, and keeps an eye on progress—or lack of it.

But Vicky moves quickly and in a different direction with Gene. Gene basically fired himself, capping a long pattern of underperformance and alcohol abuse at work with a specific instance of behavior that was egregious enough for Vicky to decide it is time for him to move on.

When people make horrendous blunders, can't learn from clear and consistent feedback, and don't respond to coaching or to role clarity, you may well be facing a challenge that goes beyond the power of a workplace intervention. In those circumstances, a clean break is best. For the sake of caring, equity, and your own peace of mind, take time to review the data, confirm you are considering the full picture, test your actions and judgments with trusted others, and reconfirm your decision.

Ask yourself if you've applied the SURE model as well as you can and have taken sufficient time and effort for a turnaround. Have you done the diagnostic work you need to do to ensure that the problem is with an individual rather than with the team or the organization? Have you looked in the mirror and identified anything you might be doing to cause or collude in the issues? Have you looked for creative ways to break patterns and alter how you and your difficult person relate to one another? Have you made sure that the individual has received consistent and sufficient feedback that describes his or her behaviors and actions, and that you have tested his or her potential for learning? Have you moved toward the individual and worked to build a relationship of sufficient trust so that you can engage in the difficult conversations and deliberate planning that performance and relationship improvement requires? Have you consulted with a trusted colleague or mentor to test your judgment? Your responsibility in life-altering decisions like this is high. Do your homework and double-check your answers!

Terminating a subordinate consistently ranks as one of the toughest tasks managers face. Few get training in how to assess employee potential for learning and develop a performance improvement plan—or in how to fire someone. But firing for good cause is sometimes necessary, and it is fateful for individuals and for organizations.

Firing is also expensive. Organizations lose experience and institutional memory, and there are always costs in hiring and training replacements. There may be procedural and legal issues at stake, so you want to ensure you understand and follow relevant laws and policies. Your HR department can help with those.

The same basic principles apply when the question is whether it's time for you to exit a failing relationship. Study the history. Ask if you've applied the SURE principles as well as you can and for long enough to make a difference. Look carefully at the costs of both staying and leaving. Test your thinking and get counsel from a trusted friend, mentor, or professional.

2. **Unhook: Facing Fear**

Vicky and Peter both confirm that unhooking is an ongoing leadership task. Deciding to fold brings its own set of unique challenges. The prospect of firing someone or terminating a relationship always triggers strong feelings, often of anxiety and ambivalence. The emotional turmoil can lead you to replay a common pattern of delaying too long and then firing—or quitting—too impulsively. You dread the prospect of trying to deal with someone who is defensive, hostile, angry, or wounded. You fear making the wrong decision, handling the process badly, or doing harm. Even with your work with the SURE model and clear justifications, you may be haunted by doubts and second guesses. Did I miss something? Did I do the right thing? Was I clear and fair? Were there no alternatives? Did I try hard enough? Should I have offered one last chance?

Dealing with bullies magnifies the indecisiveness. Their strategies are geared to undermine your confidence and clarity of mind, and the relationship may have periods of stability in which you genuinely think the worst is over.[1] Long-time bullies succeed because their ability to turn on their charm can be as strong as their behind-closed-doors attacks and manipulations—and important others may have seen only the charm.

Fear leads you to delay. The costs and stress mount, and emotions take over. Feeling frustrated, wanting to get it over with, you finally move impetuously. The fired subordinate feels blind-sided and unfairly treated. You feel a sense of failure. Your remaining subordinates wonder why you waited so long, and then did such a bad job of firing. Even if they support your decision, they wonder if you might do the same to them. Paying attention is vital when it's time to fold and take the time you need to unhook. That frees you to work through the SURE steps carefully, accept your responsibility for dealing with a serious performance issue, confront your fears, and do what you need to assure a fair and accurate decision.

Unhooking can be even harder when you struggle to decide if it's time to leave a relationship that isn't working for you. Leaving a relationship with an impossible boss raises many questions. Will you harm your career? Will you and your family suffer serious financial damage? Are you admitting defeat too soon? Should you just hang on until another job comes along? What is your responsibility to your organization: If you do not speak up, will the bullying continue for others? Does exit mean that the bully wins and you lose?

There are no easy answers. Meanwhile, you have work to do while you continue to deal with the anger, pain, and anxiety that the destructive relationship is generating. Even recognizing the price to both your health and psyche doesn't make it easier to unhook. There is a good chance that the relationship dynamics have already undermined some of your confidence in yourself and your judgment, making it even harder to sort out your best option. These are some of the toughest circumstances anyone ever faces at work. You need support and counsel from people you can trust to help you get the distance and perspective you need.

3. **Revise the Script: Prepare and Practice**

Ask yourself, "If I were comfortable and at the top of my game, how would I handle this issue?" The answer to that question can lead you to the script you need. In letting someone go, a good script communicates the decision clearly and directly. If you back into it or talk around it, you open yourself to a prolonged, unproductive debate. Once you've done your homework and decided that terminating someone is the right organizational choice, don't do anything that confuses the message or implies that it's reversible. And firing should never come as a surprise. Well before you get to that point, clear expectations, role clarity, consistent feedback, improvement plans, and accountability systems should have made it clear when someone was in final jeopardy.

This will be a difficult conversation, and do all that you can to feel balanced and comfortable during the exchange. Preparation is essential. Begin by thinking through what you want to say. Anticipate a range of possible responses to your message—including your worst fears. You'll also want to understand the feelings the conversation will evoke for you and for the other. There will be many for you both, and you don't want to be surprised by them. It's only natural for you to feel regret, sadness, anxiety, disappointment, and anger. You wouldn't be human if you didn't. Working through those in advance so as to stay focused, calm, and authentic is an important element of executive judgment[2] and wisdom.[3]

In preparing, first write out for yourself the basic message: the individual's employment will terminate at a particular time, for the following reason, and under a specified set of conditions (including any provisions for benefits, severance, out-placement, or other support). Second, express your disappointment at the outcome, and your hopes for the individual's future success. Third, give the other person a chance to respond or ask questions about your message. Write out more than one scenario and see which feels right. You'll feel more confident, give yourself flexibility in conducting the difficult meeting, and be able to respond with both clarity and care. And practice, practice, practice!

Compassion and care don't mean sugarcoating reality, though you don't want to approach the break with a sledge-hammer. Everyone needs to learn from the divorce, but a clear statement of what isn't right, what has been tried to no avail, and how to manage the transition is enough. The rules for skilled candor are a helpful guide in cases like this. It's time to let go of blame, anger, and disappointment. There's no reason to rehash everything or to use a difficult situation to reinforce your power or position.

If you have decided to leave a relationship that isn't working for you, you will face a choice of which script to follow. Paul Simon wrote that "there must be 50 ways to leave your lover," and the same is true for leaving a workplace nemesis. Sometimes, "just slip out the back, Jack" is almost all you need, particularly if a quick and clean break is your best outcome and another opportunity awaits. But leaving your employer in a lurch by not providing adequate notice could come back to haunt you. Usually you'll want to study your situation and options. What's the nature of your employment contract? What, if any, obligations does your employer have if you resign? What are your organization's usual practices when someone quits? Might you have legal claims? A friend, a mentor, and a good employment lawyer can help you sort things through. Walk through the situation with all three: each brings a different, yet vital, perspective.

4. **Engage: Be Present in the Face of Exit**

To protect yourself from the discomfort of a conversation about termination, it is tempting to distance yourself by taking a formal, bureaucratic stance: speaking in the third person ("The company has concluded. . . ."), disowning personal responsibility for the outcome ("If it were up to me alone. . . ."), or reading a script ("This is to inform you. . . ."). Termination is no time for a deep exchange of personal feelings, but you and the other person will both feel better if you are authentic in expressing your regret about the outcome and hopes for the future. Put yourself in the shoes of the other person, and treat the other as you would hope to be treated. It may be tempting as you exit a bad relationship to try to punish the other person on your way out the door. That is unlikely to give you as much satisfaction as you might hope. Aim instead for calm confidence and quiet dignity. Be your best self as you exit.

PART VI

Teamwork

20

The Game Plan

MICHAEL IS STILL IMPOSSIBLE, *but I'm feeling a lot better about everything else.* Vicky was in the same conference room where she first met her "motley crew" a month ago. She remembered being more scared than hopeful at the time. Now, she felt confident.

We're on the right track, and I think we're going to make it. That doesn't guarantee this meeting will work as well as I hope, but I'm ready. I think the team is, too. We all know the game plan.

Vicky looked at the wall clock. It was time to start. There was an air of excitement and friendly banter around the table. All present—except Michael. *Michael never makes it easy,* Vicky thought. *Shows up when I don't expect him, but not when I do. Do we wait or start without him?* Vicky took a deep breath and decided to begin.

"Good morning, everyone. Let's get started. Michael should be here soon. We've got a lot to do, so let's begin. We all know our agenda . . ."

Just then Michael burst in.

"Agenda?" he interjected. "You call this an agenda? I want numbers. What's this 'Year of the Team'?"

Vicky smiled. She'd expected Michael to toss a grenade into the meeting, and this one could have been worse. This time she was ready for him.

"Michael, we're glad you're here," Vicky responded calmly. "I figured the agenda might need some explanation and that's where we'll start."

"Better be good."

"We knew you wouldn't be satisfied with anything less," Vicky said soothingly, taking control of the meeting agenda. "We've worked hard, and we have a plan that we all feel very good about. The purpose of today's meeting is for the team to explain it to you and get your reactions. Fair enough?"

Michael looked as if he wanted a reason to say no, but couldn't find one. "So let's hear what you've got."

Vicky scanned the group. She had prepared them to ignore barbs from Michael, and they looked unfazed—except for Lin, who seemed in search of someplace to hide. Vicky caught Lin's eye and gave her a smile and slight nod of the head. Lin nodded in reply. *Come on team! We've practiced our lines,* Vicky told herself. *We're ready. Let's get on with it.*

"I'll give a brief overview," Vicky continued on and with a smile, "then turn it over to members of the team to talk about specifics. Starting with the big picture. We've done a lot in the last month. We know past results have been unacceptable. We now agree on what needs to be fixed. We have a plan for going forward, and we're committing to aggressive targets. You'll start seeing better numbers in the next quarter. For the year, we expect to be above forecast."

"Up on profits or revenues?" Michael growled.

"Both, Michael. Lin will present the specifics later in the meeting."

"How is this motley crew going to pull off a miracle?"

The team let Michael's barbs go by—like water through open fingers.

"Execution, speed, and teamwork, Michael," Vicky answered quickly and calmly. "And we realize that we can't do the first two without the last. That's why we're calling it *The Year of the Team.* Madison will start by talking about sales."

"Thanks for the good overview, Vicky," Madison responded, exuding her usual charm and professionalism. "The vacancy in sales gave us a chance to talk as a full team about what we need. We're looking for a team player with a strong technical background. That will help us sell our newer products and respond more quickly to customers. For the moment, Vicky and I are sharing oversight of the sales function, and I appreciate the opportunity it's giving me to learn. With input from the full team, we've put together a job description, and we expect to make a new hire within the month. I'm happy to answer any questions."

"How much are we going to pay this guy?" Michael asked.

"Might not be a guy, Michael, but we're lucky that right now there are good candidates," Madison replied warmly. "We think we'll get a strong hire without paying more than we were paying Gene."

Michael grunted, maybe in satisfaction, though it wasn't easy to tell. Vicky picked up the ball and immediately passed it to the next player.

"Next, Nathan will talk about engineering. Nathan?"

"Okay. Thanks, Vicky," Nathan cleared his throat and continued. "Frankly, if Vicky hadn't come, I probably would have quit. I'd rather design than manage anyway, particularly the way things were going around here—I never got any support and the signals kept changing. I never knew what to believe. Damn near impossible to do good work. But now Madison, Carlos, and I worked together studying our markets. The truth is, we should have done that a long time ago. We found some openings out there that we just weren't seeing before."

Nathan paused to make eye contact with Madison and Carlos. The slight smile on his face indicated he was enjoying himself. He then continued.

"Maybe I should have known this sooner, but I didn't. We've been overdesigning, putting in features our customers don't care about and missing some simple things they do want. So our prices have been too high, and we've been late to market. The good news is we've got a technical edge because my group knows some stuff our competitors don't. So, you want a miracle, Michael? How about better products, faster, at a lower cost?"

"You sure about that?" Michael asked skeptically but with some of the steam gone from his voice.

"Very. It's already speeding up our design work. And it's going to make things easier down the line for Carlos, too."

"Perfect transition," Vicky interjected, keeping the pace crisp. "Carlos, you're up next."

"Basically, I'm singing the same tune you've heard from Madison and Nathan. We're on the same page more than we've ever been. The market study helped us all see a lot of ways that engineering and production can work together so that our products not only work better, they're easier to make. The consultant Vicky brought in helped a lot, too. Gave me a whole new perspective on my job and the operation. We've launched a Six Sigma program, and we're already starting to see improvements in speed and quality."

"Words are cheap. What have you guys been smoking?" Michael scoffed.

Vicky was ready. *Our dragon is on script, breathing fire on cue,* she thought to herself.

"Of course, you have some doubts, Michael," Vicky said soothingly. "We understand that results are the only thing that will convince you. That takes us to the last item on our agenda. Lin is going to give you the numbers, tell you our targets. They're ambitious. Lift-off won't come for a few months, and then things will start to accelerate. By a year from now, they'll be a lot better. And you'll know if we did what we said. But don't be too surprised if we beat them. Lin?"

"Thanks, Vicky," Lin began softly. "We've developed a performance dashboard. It took some work. I've got it all on one page. I'll pass that out now. It includes process measures that will give us early signals of whether we're on track, as well as outcome measures—units sold, revenue, net, and so on."

"Let me add," interjected Madison when Lin finished, "one thing that's new. I'll be the first to admit it wasn't easy, but we've agreed that we're all accountable for all the measures. We win or lose as a team."

"So if this is so easy, why didn't you figure it out a hell of a lot sooner?" Michael asked.

A silence fell over the room. Vicky deliberately passed on the opportunity to answer for the team.

Finally, Madison spoke up. "You want the truth, Michael?"

"What else would I want?"

"Okay. The truth is there's been a climate of fear and hostility around here. Dog-eat-dog, everyone looking out for themselves, blaming problems on someone else. It wasn't until Vicky came that we realized that's why we were failing. Now we see that we can win as a team if we all do our part. It may sound corny, but it's exciting! The last month has been the most fun I've had at work in a long time."

Carlos, Lin, and Nathan smiled and shook their heads yes as she spoke.

Interlude 6

A SURE Tour de Force

IT IS NO SURPRISE THAT MICHAEL SEES the team's plan as a mirage pretending to be a miracle. The team is asking him to trust a process that, by all indications, violates both his beliefs about how to manage and motivate people and what is possible from this group of employees. Why should he believe that the "motley crew" will do better than it ever has before? They have a history of failure; and even Michael's browbeating, threats, and firing of their multiple bosses have done nothing to change that. That is, until Vicky came.

Vicky brings another approach to managing people, and she and her team have achieved something remarkable. They have found a path to success under difficult circumstances. There is much to learn from how they did it. Vicky has consistently relied on the principles in the SURE model, and she has coached her team on the *rules of engagement* so that they can begin to do the same.

1. **Stop, Look, and Learn: Step Back, Step Up, Step It Up**

   Vicky's first move in her new job is to study the business and the players. The business results have been disappointing, and careful diagnostic work allows her to see that the problems are more about a failure of teamwork, adequate support, and clear expectations. She sets out to work on that. Vicky also knows that she'll solve the teamwork problem only if she finds ways to alter the climate of fear and ragtag individualism created by Michael's erratic, punitive management style.

Vicky asks her team to stop, look, and learn—engaging in discussions to help her understand the current state and future possibilities in their areas. Team members take a fresh look with her help, and all learn new ways to understand themselves and their areas. Vicky brings her consistent calm persistence, but individualizes her approach to each member of her team: Madison gets multiple invitations to step up followed by confrontation; Lin, continuous encouragement and soft suggestions; Carlos, some combination of these. Vicky demonstrates a new model of leading: step back and study, then step things up.

Vicky also offers each a tempting carrot in contrast to Michael's wide-swinging stick: Lin, a strategy for impact; Carlos, training and vital data; Madison, a route to promotion. Vicky stays close to each individual to support learning and offer new ways of working, but she does not micromanage. She assigns team projects that require collaboration, like the joint analysis of the unit's markets. She gives the team space and timelines, and holds it responsible to do the work, which leads them to discover new business insights and the benefits of teamwork. Nathan's report to Michael confirms they found both.

A Dallas turnaround requires adaptive change for the team, and leadership that fosters it.[1] The same ways of working that got the unit into its current troubles will not get it out.[2] Vicky creates opportunities for team members to discover and embrace different strategies and solutions they have been hard-pressed to see before—and to grow and develop professionally as they work. Madison's testimonial on the power of shared responsibility bodes well for the team's future.

2. **Unhook: Use and Teach**

One of Vicky's biggest challenges is unhooking from the toxic stew Michael is so good at generating. She uses several strategies. One is disciplining herself to avoid quick and impetuous reactions to Michael's provocations. She demonstrates this in her very first meeting with him when "she paused, struggling to tamp down an impulse to scream that Michael was a thug, and she'd rather work for any other boss in the world." She takes the time to come up with something better than screaming at her boss. After pausing, she asks, "What can you tell me about the team I'm inheriting?" That response illustrates another strategy that helps Vicky unhook: ask a question instead of saying something stupid. A third strategy is to seek counsel from a trusted advisor. She is fortunate to have a wise and supportive mentor in Peter. If you don't have a Peter in your life, look for one!

Michael is an equal opportunity abuser, and Vicky knows that she must teach the team to unhook and be there for them when they face the dragon's flame. It could not have been pleasant for any of them to have their boss's boss send random, negative, and unhelpful feedback on their efforts.

3. **Revise the Script: Do and Teach**

Even before Vicky arrives in the Dallas office, she understands that she faces a challenge ripe for failure: a notoriously difficult boss and a failing operation. She cannot succeed if she lets the pressures in the situation push her to repeat the same patterns of failure. Revising the script is her only hope for success. Vicky creates a new script for dealing with Michael, whose punitive style must have pushed her predecessors into reactive self-protection or fury. She also writes a new script for working with her subordinates that emphasizes information, teamwork, support, and trust—rather than demands and threats. But that is not enough. Vicky also needs to guide the team to revise their current scripts for dealing with their jobs, their boss, each other—and Michael.

4. **Engage Deeply: Evolve or Exit**

Vicky consistently chooses to engage both Michael and her team. Michael's fire-breathing style is well designed to frighten and keep people off-balance: "Stay back or you might get burned!" Vicky understands that it is better to engage on her terms than continually react to Michael's. So she works to initiate and engage with a strategy built around transparency, no surprises, specific commitments, and realistic optimism. Her commitment to make Michael look good is key to her approach. She takes initiative and makes offers that are hard for Michael to refuse, much as he might like. If Michael continues to say no to things that are clearly and rationally in his best interest, Vicky learns something important. If Michael is beyond reasonable influence, it may be time to document and consider her exit options.

PART VII

A Happy Ending?

21

The New Boss

EIGHTEEN MONTHS AFTER ARRIVING AT the Dallas office, Vicky tapped lightly on the frame of the open office door. "Got a minute?"

Michael looked up. "Not really." He turned back to the files on his desk as Vicky entered the office and took a seat. She waited for him to look up.

"What's your problem now?" Michael said before looking down again at his work.

"Michael, I've been offered another job and I'm going to take it."

He looked up. "Not too surprised. I toughen you up and someone else benefits. Sorry I'll miss your farewell party."

"I've learned a lot in Dallas, and I feel good about what we've been able to do."

"So who's the lucky suitor?" Michael said as he again looked down at the work in front of him.

"I'm going to Corporate, Michael. Head of North American operations. There'll be a formal announcement next Monday. I want to tell the team beforehand."

Michael looked up. Vicky had never seen him so completely stunned. His cheeks grew red as her words sunk in. When he spoke, his anger was barely controlled. "I've been working my butt off here for eight years. Six operations. Fighting fire after fire. You come in and jump over me, and get the job I want. How the hell did you do that, sister?"

"That's a good question. A short answer is that it was part of a plan that I didn't know about. They figured if I could make a go of this job, I'd be ready for something bigger. I want to talk about that. We also need to talk about transition."

"Oh, yeah. Or should I say, anything you want." He paused. "Boss."

"That would be the old Michael speaking. I'm hoping for the new Michael with a bright future. That's who I want to work with."

Michael stared at her as if her words made no sense. His scowl deepened and his face got even redder. Vicky had the sense of being in a small room with an angry, wounded beast that might attack at any moment. She felt tense and gave herself time to quiet the inner turmoil. Finally, she spoke again.

"Michael, you're the most challenging boss I've ever worked for."

"So you can't take the heat and you're getting out of the kitchen."

"Well, at first I didn't know if I could stand the heat. Corporate didn't know either. That's one of the reasons they put me here. To test my resolve and resilience. Like, if I could work well with you, I could deal with anything."

Vicky knew she was telling Michael things he had heard before, but she still watched carefully for his response.

"Hell, yeah, I'm tough. That's what got me where I am."

Vicky paused before responding. *Slow and gentle,* she told herself. "And are you also aware it's what kept you here?"

Michael stared at her, mouth open. Vicky waited.

"What in the hell are you talking about?"

"Michael, you want to be successful, and I want you to be successful. You're as smart and knowledgeable about this industry as anyone in the company."

"So," he said, disgust in his voice, "then tell me why *you're* getting the promotion."

"Have you noticed that your results have improved, since we started working together?"

"And of course you're taking full credit for that?"

Vicky paused again. "I said we, not me. That might be the biggest difference between us."

Michael looked puzzled. "What are you talking about?"

"Michael, you don't say 'we' very often. I think your results will be better if you start thinking and saying it more."

"Oh, I get it," Michael responded, making no effort to hide the sarcasm. "*We* just sit around, hold hands, and all talk nice. Work gets done by itself, eh?" Michael pushed over the stack of folders on his desk, and they scattered across it. A few fell to the floor, and he left them there.

"People see me as optimistic, Michael. But I hope they don't get the impression that I'm soft or naïve. Optimism works for me. So does respect and engagement. I find when I expect good things from people and treat them as I would like to be treated, they usually come through. I'm hoping for the same with you."

Michael was silent. Vicky waited until he spoke again. "Don't hold your breath," he finally said.

"No need. I expect we'll be seeing a lot of each other. This office is headed in a good direction. We need to keep that going. Let's plan to meet on transition issues. The team will want to know next steps. I have two specific agenda items for that meeting. You may have others. I'll want your thoughts on whether Madison is ready for my job, and how we'll assure that the team continues to get the support it needs."

"I'm booked solid for the next few days or so. I'll have Sandy set up a meeting when I'm more open next week."

"Let's try for day after tomorrow, Michael. This is important enough to find an opening. Can you check your calendar now for what you can reschedule? We'll want a full hour."

As she left his office, Vicky knew there was no guarantee of success with Michael. There might come a time when it would be necessary to part ways. But, annoying as he was, Michael had talent and experience. How much of what she was seeing—Michael's negativity, defensiveness, unpredictable barbs—is him, and how much is situational? With better coaching and clearer expectations, could engagement work even with Michael? Vicky wasn't ready to give up yet.

EPILOGUE
THE SURE ROUTE TO SUCCESS: ENGAGEMENT

That is what learning is. You suddenly understand
something you've understood all your life,
but in a new way.

—Doris Lessing

AS THE CURTAIN FALLS ON OUR WORKPLACE SAGA, Vicky is moving up, and Michael is stuck in the same job, wondering, *Why her and not me?* Part of the answer is Vicky's skill and savvy in orchestrating a turnaround where others had failed. She brought openness, determination, and good diagnostic skills to the *deep engagement* of the difficult and underperforming people she inherited. A turnaround takes teamwork, even for the most skilled and experienced of leaders.

Vicky began by clarifying if she had the right people for her team, affirming their commitment—or arranging their exit—and creating the right conditions for each to bring their best to the work. What looked like a transformational miracle of a motley crew was at its core deep engagement and skilled application of proven principles for workplace success: separating people from the problem, identifying individual capabilities and needs, testing assumptions, clarifying roles and expectations, providing support and coaching, fostering new understandings of oneself and others, treating people with respect and professionalism (and asking for the same in return), setting clear goals and holding people accountable for them, addressing problems in a timely manner, moving toward difficult people—not away, and modeling healthy ways to self-manage and unhook in the face of stress and strain. The *rules of engagement* guided Vicky in her efforts.

A second part of the answer to Michael's question is the skill and savvy Vicky brought to the challenge of working for a bully. She showed *courageous engagement:* crafting and testing strategies for working and coping with a very difficult individual in the context of a boss-subordinate role and power structure. The turnaround would have been impossible without that, as would Vicky's—and her team's—health and sanity.

Vicky's skills and accomplishments before she arrived in Dallas had earned her another vital asset—she had allies. These included friends in high places like headquarters executives who offered her opportunities for growth and promotion, and her mentor and former boss, Peter. They also included colleagues like the networks she tapped to prepare for Dallas. Over time, Vicky turned her team into strong allies—and Vicky's strong external support was a key to Madison's decision to join rather than oppose her. Vicky knows the importance of good *political engagement* skills: she knows how to make allies and is not hesitant to reach out to them. If this is less true for you, ask how you could begin to change that.

Strong allies gave Vicky political assets that targets of bullying often lack. Vicky had powerful protectors, like Peter, who listened in a context of support, respect, and first-hand knowledge of her work. Although Vicky did not know it when she took on Dallas, Corporate had plans for her. A signal from Peter to parachute her—or Michael—out should the situation become destructive gave her vital political cover. Targets of bullies often go it alone and come to be seen as poor performers or disgruntled whistleblowers. Their coworkers often abandon them or side with the bully for self-protection. Inadequate responses from HR or senior management[1] add to the challenge. If Vicky had not had strong allies, her story might have had a more dismal ending.[2]

The solitary superhero is a staple in film and fiction, but going it alone is rarely a strategy for success in the work world—particularly in the face of hostility and bullying. Success and sanity are much easier to achieve when you nurture a network of support—your tribe[3]—to be there for you.

In the contrast between Vicky and Michael, we also see the fruits of two distinct models of people management that are widely found at work and elsewhere. Each model sometimes works, but Vicky's is a better bet in the modern workplace. Michael's style has served him well enough to get him where he is, but has kept him from progressing further. Vicky has passed him on the road to career success following principles of *collaborative engagement* that respond to critical requirements in twenty-first-century organizations: the capacity to solve hard problems in a complex and volatile world, work effectively in a world of enduring differences, build high-performing teams, and bring out the best in individual contributors.

Michael's approach to people is built on classic beliefs that employees work best when they are tightly controlled, closely monitored, and motivated more with stick than carrot. It's captured by an old cartoon line, "The beatings will continue until performance improves." Built on principles of self-interest, competition, and motivating through fear, it sees workers and relationships simply as tools to be used for the end of getting work done. People who follow this model see themselves as tough and realistic survivors in a cutthroat world. Sometimes, in some circumstances, they're right. But those times and places are fading into the past: the old ways don't work as well as they used to.

Vicky's approach is geared to the fast-paced, turbulent, diverse, technology-infused, and complex global world facing modern managers. In that world, the traditional model of concentrating decisions at the top and expecting everyone below to do what they're told creates more problems than it solves. Decision-makers at the top can't keep up because too much is happening too fast. They can never get all the information they need to make timely decisions, nor can they bring all the creativity and innovation essential for adapting to the fast pace of change. What works now is empowering and supporting capable decision-makers at every level—encouraging everyone to lead and make good decisions whether they are sitting at the head or the foot of the table. That's why Vicky's approach to people emphasizes empowerment; valid information; strong teams; collaborative problem solving; and engaging people in challenging tasks that use their diverse knowledge, experience, perspectives, and expertise.

Vicky's approach is also underpinned by a respect for the human capacity to learn and develop when encouraged and supported to do so. She could have written off her motley crew, who had failed under multiple bosses. Their approach to work and to one another seemed more self-centered and idiosyncratic than geared toward shared goals or the bottom line. Vicky's own career was on the line. Who would have blamed her for wanting a clean slate and new talent?

But Vicky understands something important about human nature and relationships. People almost never choose to fail, but sometimes they are in situations that make it very hard for them to succeed. Or they may perpetuate old habits of thought and action that no longer serve them well. Vicky knows that what has been learned can be unlearned. With a mind-set of optimism, strong belief in the human capacity to grow, and clear *rules of engagement,* Vicky set out to provide her team members with opportunities to rise to their personal best. She accepted that the work would be hard and would require patience, focus, and persistence. But her willingness to engage people with respect, clear expectations, and honest feedback made a difference—for the business, for Vicky and her career, and for each member of the crew. Vicky's closing comments to Michael demonstrate the strength of her beliefs in human potential.

The SURE Principles: Remember the Basics

Vicky's success illustrates the power of our four *rules of engagement.* In earlier sections, we discussed how the principles apply to many of the toughest people challenges you will encounter. Here, we review them with a focus on why they work.

1. **Stop, Look, and Learn (Before You Leap)**
   Doing what you already know often works for problems you've seen before and know how to solve. When you run into a new challenge, it's tempting to move fast to clear the ever-full plate so you can get to the next item awaiting your attention. Solving familiar problems quickly is a basic management skill, but pros also know how to spot the black swans and solve the

hard stuff. That is what sets you apart from the crowd. That work requires open, flexible, and deliberate habits of the mind.

These habits inform our Rule 1: take the time to look (and learn) when you find yourself facing stubborn, messy situations in which it's hard to know what's *really* going on and what you can do about it. In a work world that often rewards snap judgments—even bad ones—it takes discipline and effort to develop the kind of systematic approach to understanding self, others, and situations that Vicky illustrates. It also takes courage, workable strategies, and finesse to withstand pressures from bosses like Michael when they insist that you see the world as they do, do what they tell you, and get it done fast.

Sense-making is the difficult art at the heart of solving difficult people problems. It involves three basic steps: notice something, decide what to make of it, and determine what to do about it. Humans are pretty good at all three, but we do them so automatically that we can easily overlook three important—and limiting—features of the process.

1. Sense-making is incomplete and personal. In any given situation, you can attend to only a portion of the available information. You notice some things, ignore others, and draw conclusions—and these steps occur so fast you barely know they are happening. For that reason, your conclusions feel more like *Truth* and the way the world really is than the personal interpretations they are. So you see little need to question your interpretations or retrace the steps you took to reach them.

2. Sense-making is interpretive and self-sealing. When thrown into life's ongoing stream of experiences, you create explanations of what things mean—and often assume that others either see things the same way or, if they don't, they are wrong. Once you've developed your interpretation, you'll often defend rather than test it. That can lead to stubbornly insisting you're right even though you aren't getting the results you want.

3. Sense-making is prescriptive and action-oriented. Your personal interpretations contain implicit prescriptions for how

you and others should respond. If, for example, you agreed with Madison's assessment that Carlos is a lost cause, you'll fire him. If you believe improved morale is the path to increased productivity, you'll value him. It's easy to be off and running before you're sure what's happening and where you should *really* be heading.

"We carve out order by leaving the disorderly parts out," concludes eminent psychologist William James;[4] and we're rarely aware that this is what we are doing. When we get things wrong, we're in a bind—would we rather flip-flop or defend something that's wrong?

You increase your ability to get it right by taking the time to stop, look, and learn using strategies we've discussed, like study your challenge, analyze people in context, and understand others' problems and pressures.

2. **Unhook (To Get Free)**

Whenever you face a stubborn challenge and nothing seems to work, unhooking offers a path to freedom. Unhooking is the process of letting go of assumptions, automatic emotional responses, and old habits that keep you stuck. When things go wrong, it is tempting to protect your self-esteem by insisting that you're fine just as you are, and someone else is responsible for your problems. That makes it hard to see your responsibility for failed interactions. As a result, you don't see other options and the need to search for them. You get caught in the same emotional stew and repeat the same ineffective behaviors again and again. It happens to us all—and more than we realize. It is particularly common in the most stressful and challenging situations that we encounter, and difficult people problems fall into that category. The result is that we may handle routine interactions with aplomb, but flounder with those that demand our best.

Mentors or friends can help you unhook. It is easier to learn about the gaps between your intention and impact[5] when others take the time to help you see them. That's the power of honest feedback. It's a cornerstone for personal and professional growth, and trying to fix people problems without understanding what you may contribute to them is a recipe for failure. Looking in the mirror—separating what's you from what's other people, taking responsibility, and facing fear—gives you the insights you need to learn about yourself, see new possibilities for effective interaction with others, and be confident in them.

3. **Revise the Script (Change and Others Will, Too)**

If you keep doing what you've always done, others will probably do the same, and you'll all stay stuck in whatever morass you're in. Relationships are like a dance and are built on the same general rules: partners move together in an agreed-upon pattern, influenced by the rhythm and steps of whoever is leading. As Peter reminds Vicky, if you change how you lead the dance—how you interact with others—they will probably respond differently. Strategies we've discussed—like understanding and speaking openly about hot-button issues (and working to get beyond their tacit grasp), interrupting unproductive scripts, and offering solutions rather than problems—get you on a more creative and satisfying path. New behaviors are just that, so write out different scenarios for yourself. Before you use them, practice; then practice some more.

4. **Engage (Lean in, Move Closer)**

Complicated, fast-paced work environments increase the frequency and the importance of people problems because they require individuals from different places with different experiences, styles, backgrounds, and perspectives to come together and figure out quickly how to get things done. Differences lead to divergent interpretations of what's going on, what's important, and what we should do, yet interdependence means that we have to deal with one another and find common ground. The stage is set for discomfort, confusion, and conflict, much as we might like seamless collaboration. We'll fail if we start to pull away from each other whenever differences surface and relationships get hard.

We need instead to understand and practice basic ways of moving closer. We need to proactively engage and learn from one another through inquiry and skilled candor. Engagement at its core is partnering, befriending, and acknowledging the richness of our humanity. Exploring differences and staying the course when it gets difficult—as Vicky demonstrates in her interactions with Michael—provides the crucibles in which we can learn about the trade-offs among our competing goals and perspectives, and from which we will find innovative solutions to tough problems.

In comparing Vicky and Michael, we see that successful engagement is built on finesse, not force. Force may get you what you want in the short term, but it creates enemies and throws sand in the gears of relationships and collective problem-solving. It invites unproductive, win-lose battles over who's right, not what's right. Those who use force rarely get the feedback they need to see the negative impact of their strategies because their behavior pushes people away and into self-protection mode. When Madison told Michael in Chapter 20 that "The truth is there's been a climate of fear and hostility around here," it was the first time one of his subordinates found the courage to tell him that his style had created a workplace that eroded motivation and fed needless competition. In such a world, no one takes responsibility for much beyond looking out for oneself.

In contrast, finesse takes subtlety and artistry. It requires savvy and a range of interpersonal skills [many that we discuss in detail in the next section, *Skills of Engagement*]. In any environment that puts a premium on collaboration and good teamwork, success goes to those who know how to practice relationship jiujutsu, ask for help, pose good questions to facilitate reflection and creative problem solving, and communicate with clarity and respect.

Successful engagement builds trust, which is at the core of effective relationships. People who cannot trust one another will have trouble doing anything together. Those who do trust can accomplish great things. Individuals who tell the truth, deliver on commitments, listen actively, avoid unpleasant surprises, and keep promises, build the trust they need to work effectively across boundaries and over time.

CONCLUSION

Harold Pinter won a Nobel Prize for brilliant plays that probe the complexities and frailties of human interaction. He once wrote, "Communication is too alarming. To enter into someone else's life is too frightening. To disclose to others the poverty within us is too fearsome a possibility."[6] His words capture all too well the doubts and fears that keep people apart and undermine their ability to work with others. Because those deep fears and doubts will always be with you, the work of building effective relationships will never be easy. That is why the principles in the SURE model are so valuable. They provide a compass to guide you to a safe harbor amid a daunting and messy interpersonal storm. They provide direction when you feel befogged. Sail on! Hard as it will sometimes be, the journey to bring your best self to your relationships—and to help others do the same—is worth the effort.

THE SKILLS OF ENGAGEMENT TUTORIAL

SUCCESSFUL USE OF THE SURE MODEL DEPENDS on skillful application of the four *rules of engagement* and of the foundational skills, practices, and habits of mind that underpin them.

The action moves quickly in our story, and in the interludes we discuss what we see unfolding. This tutorial digs more deeply into the *how to* behind the strategies and choices Vicky exemplifies and into *how you* can begin to add each in new or deeper ways to your professional repertoire. Our "Try This" suggestions get you started, and there are plenty of references in the footnotes to enable deeper study.

The tutorial serves as a handy primer for identifying specific skills that can be combined to transform difficult relationships at work. This section covers a lot of ground and might feel overwhelming if you try to take it all in at one go. Use it instead as a reference. Return to it periodically to brush up old skills or acquire new ones. Dip into it when you are looking for ideas about how to handle particular challenges or when you feel your current strategies aren't taking you where you need to go.

We use the four *rules of engagement* to organize the materials, and provide a summary chart for your convenience. Not every skill or habit, however, fits neatly in only one category.

Inquiry, for example, is discussed as a building block for the first rule **(stop, look, and learn)**. But inquiry can also be a way to unhook.

We see Vicky asking Michael questions to deflect his caustic barbs and stay focused on her goals. She also uses inquiry and different kinds of questions to be more confronting in conversations with team members—revising her initial scripts, for example, in her second meetings with Madison and Carlos.

Developing skills or habits requires more than just reading about them. As with learning to play basketball or the saxophone, virtuoso performance requires sustained effort, learning from mistakes, exercises to stretch technique, and practice over time. Our goal here is to encourage you to inventory your own repertoire of relationship skills to explore those that you want to develop or enhance. Once you've set learning goals, you can start practicing, reflect on your progress, find ways to add to what you know, and then practice some more. Instruction and further reading can accelerate the process, but the old adage is still true: experience is the best teacher.

SURE *Rules of Engagement*	Skills, Practices, and Habits of the Mind
Stop, Look, and Learn	Inquiry
	Testing
	Thinking gray and free
	Informed compassion
Unhook	Reflection and journaling
	Consulting
	Mindful vigilance
	Enhancing resilience, building mental strength
	Joyful attention training
Revise the Script	Generating options
	Creating scenarios
	Humor
Engage—Evolve or Exit	Skilled candor
	Giving and receiving good feedback

STOP, LOOK, AND LEARN

Inquiry

Always the beautiful answer/Who asks a more beautiful question.[1]

—e. e. cummings

We start with inquiry for a reason. It is foundational for learning, problem solving, innovation, personal and professional growth, and relationship building. Good questions can change lives and the course of history, and the resolution of big and thorny social problems requires them. Few are taught in their professional training to ask good questions or to fully appreciate the benefits. Journalists may be the rare exception.[2]

We concentrate here on inquiry as an interpersonal skill to foster better exchanges with the difficult people in your life, but note the value and importance of the questions you ask—or don't ask—to yourself.

Inquiry seeks to discover or learn what others think, know, want, or feel. The basic inquiry skill is knowing how to ask good questions. Good questions typically begin with words like *how, why,* or *what.* They go beyond asking for a *yes* or *no* response. They encourage people instead to provide information, describe their thinking, explore ideas, share their perspective, or consider new possibilities. Good inquiry is necessary for testing ideas, seeking feedback, learning from others, and situational diagnosis. As we note at several points in Vicky's story, inquiry also serves as a skillful alternative to advocacy—a gentle way to ask someone to consider an idea or a possibility that he or she might otherwise resist. This can be a win-win for both parties, as they learn from one another and see new options. Tightly connected to good inquiry is active and attentive listening. The benefits of inquiry are lost if others see it as a technique and not a route to deeper understanding.

Edgar Schein defines "humble inquiry"[3] as the fine art of asking others questions based on your curiosity and sincere interest in them. The purpose is to draw others out and into a closer and more trusting relationship. Schein sees humble inquiry as an investment of time and attention to build foundations for effective teamwork.

Inquiry is a habit of the mind that does not come easily to everyone, especially in a world that values experts who have answers. Business organizations often view questions as "inefficient" and the antithesis of action, task completion, and forward momentum, according to Clayton Christensen,[4] an advocate of good questions as a way to foster disruptive innovation. The image of the charismatic extrovert—someone who speaks out and speaks up—still dominates everyday beliefs about effective and powerful leadership.[5]

Try This

Enhancing your inquiry skills suggests attention to two areas: (1) increasing your use of questions, and (2) asking better questions. Start by seeing where you are on each.

1. *Compare your advocacy and inquiry counts:* Over the course of the next week, be mindful in your conversations with others about the balance between your advocacy (telling) and your inquiry (asking). Take time after a number of selected conversations to think about: How many questions did you ask the other versus how many statements did you make? Tracking your ratio of advocacy and inquiry allows you to work on changing the balance.

2. *Descriptive questions:* Take as a goal for a day or a time to avoid asking questions that seek a *yes* or *no* answer. Substitute instead questions that begin with *how, why,* or *what.* How easy is that for you? How does that change the tenor of your conversations? Why do you think that is? What have you learned about others as a result?

Testing

Better thinking is a key to interpersonal effectiveness—and great leadership.[7] You increase your chances of relating well to others

> Your assumptions are your windows on the world. Scrub them off every once in a while, or the light won't come in.[6]
> —*Alan Alda*

and achieving the results you want when you understand how natural features in human cognition can get you into trouble. The *Ladder of Inference,* developed by Chris Argyris,[8] can help. It is a set of ideas worthy of deeper study and at the core of the organizational learning movement, furthered by the work of Peter Senge.[9]

The *Ladder of Inference* basically describes the thinking process you go through, usually without realizing it, in moving from perception to action. From the pool of all the directly observable data around you, you notice certain things and ignore others. You then move one step up the ladder and decide what the data means—you interpret it based on your existing knowledge, beliefs, and preferences. Moving up another step, you draw conclusions about how you should respond to the meaning that you see. The whole process happens very fast, usually outside of awareness.

What's important for our purpose here is to recognize how quickly and tacitly you can jump from fact to action—from the bottom rung of the ladder to the top—unaware of the ways your choices, beliefs, experiences, assumptions, and inferences may have led you to wrong conclusions along the way. Your personal interpretations feel like truth to you—but may not be. That's why testing is vital.

People often believe or assert things that are not true, and get into trouble by acting as if they were. One of the skills that Vicky demonstrates often during her early days in Dallas is a systematic and persistent approach to testing ideas that she is hearing or developing. As she formulates hypotheses about the members of her team, she looks for ways to get additional information that would help her test which ones she should retain and which ones she should drop.

The concept of testing can also be very useful as a way to deal with disagreement. When people differ, they often get into an unproductive "I'm right, you're wrong" exchange. It's more productive to name the disagreement (for example: "We don't agree about whether Madison can become a real team player") and then to ask, "What could we do or what information would we need to collect that would enable us to test our different assumptions?"

Testing is also a way to worry less about what others are thinking, or why they may be behaving in the way that they do. Just ask them!

Try This

Use the *Ladder of Influence* to slow down your thinking and to become more disciplined in recognizing when you are making assumptions and of the need to test them. Once you've strengthened those habits of the mind, you can include more active testing into your conversations with others. Exercises to try include:

1. Use the *Ladder of Inference* to reflect on how you are thinking about a difficult person or situation by asking yourself questions that parallel the *Ladder's* rungs, like:

   - Am I considering all the facts? What might I be forgetting?

   - How am I thinking about the information I have? What's influencing me?

   - What assumptions am I making about what I see or hear, and how are they influencing the story I am telling myself?

   - Why do I believe my decision is the right thing to do?

   - What alternatives do I have?

2. Ask others to join you in using the *Ladder of Influence* as a way to deeply engage them in conversations to test your own thinking and to better understand theirs. Questions listed above are a good starting point. You signal the desire to better understand others, and present a useful model for approaching difficult situations going forward.

Thinking Gray and Free

Difficult people are difficult because what usually works with others in a similar situation does not work with them. For that reason, you need to harness your creative best and identify fresh options for breakthroughs in your difficult relationships. Thinking gray and free[11] can help you break out of your cognitive ruts!

> It's not that I'm so smart. But I stay with the questions much longer.[10]
> —*Albert Einstein*

It is easy and almost automatic to rush to judgment in dealing with new information or situations by labeling them good or bad or right or wrong or true or false. Difficult relationships are stressful; and fast, decisive action is one way to relieve the stress. But in dealing with a difficult relationship, snap judgments may put you on a dead-end road. Thinking that you are right and the other is wrong, you keep doing what you've always done while hoping the other person will change. Relationships rarely work that way. To "**stop, look, and learn**," you need to slow life down and come to grips with its nuances and complexities. We saw Vicky work hard to avoid snap judgments that could block her ability to fully assess the situation, learn about herself and others, and contemplate her range of options.

When asked, managers often say that they try to "consider all the options" before reaching a difficult decision. Steven Sample disagrees.[12] Managers may consider all their options, but do so within the constraints of their current thinking patterns and approaches. Learning to think gray and free is "an unnatural act" that forces you well beyond your comfort zone to avoid reaching any conclusion on a topic and as a result tap into your unused cognitive pathways for creative insights. As you move beyond the temptation to plow ahead and fix things, you will also see more clearly what matters — and what doesn't.

Sample's favorite way to stimulate that kind of thinking is to contemplate problems in absolutely outrageous and impossible ways. The process of arriving at his highly successful patent design for a dishwasher control,[13] for example, reads like something from a Charlie Chaplin movie: Sample crawled on the ground to contemplate the controls from different angles and forced himself to imagine controlling a dishwasher with a French horn, sofa, ladybugs, electrons, hay bales, and more. This thinking was so difficult that he could sustain it for only about 10 minutes at a time. But after a few of these thinking sessions, he suddenly saw in his mind's eye the complete circuit design — and a way to do it he had never contemplated before.

Warren Berger suggests asking yourself different kinds of questions to spark unexpected insights and breakthroughs.[14] Replace, for example, the conventional *What should I do?* with *Why is this an issue? Why do I see this as a problem? What if I tried this?* and

How else might I do it? Innovation comes when you challenge your assumptions and allow yourself to revel in blue-sky moments when anything is possible.

Try This

Steven Sample uses various techniques to stretch his capabilities to think gray and free. Two favorites are described here.[15] Try one!

1. *Resist the temptation for binary thinking:* Force yourself to read an article, listen to a news report, or engage in a conversation with another and suspend *all* judgments: don't believe or disbelieve, or classify anything as right or wrong. Listen and keep telling yourself, "that's really interesting." If you find you can't, then write down your first impression about the matter, and force yourself to not think about it until a later time (or ever again). Training your mind to "bend over backward by thinking gray with respect to a few everyday matters" is an excellent way to overcome your natural inclinations to judge and to think in a *yes* or *no* fashion.[16]

2. *Contemplate the outrageous together:* Gather a group of people who have widely varying perspectives and a common goal. Ask each individual to propose an off-the-wall idea for achieving the goal, with the proviso that every other person in the group must respond with at least two reasons why the idea will work.[17] There is a benefit in forcing yourself to learn to think positively and deeply about an idea you'd rather quickly reject.

Informed Compassion

Compassion does not mean feeling sorry for people or inviting the world's suffering into your living room: it is attunement to others with the hope that through your intentional interactions with them,

> You must not hate those who do wrong or harmful things; but with compassion, you must do what you can to stop them.
> —*Dalai Lama XIV*

their suffering is diminished.[18] Compassion at its core is inviting others into your circle: offering to understand them and working to be kind even when you disagree with what they do or believe. In the language of our book, compassion is a pillar of *courageous engagement.* We add the adjective "informed" to underscore that compassion is not denial or collusion. It is an authentic expression of deep human connection and a belief that all can learn.

The Dalai Lama, the world's symbol of compassion, sees its expression as self-serving with additional benefits to others and society at large.

> Compassion is what makes our lives meaningful. It is the source of all lasting happiness and joy. And it is the foundation of a good heart, the heart of one who acts out of a desire to help others. Through kindness, through affection, through honesty, through truth and justice toward others we ensure our own benefit. This is not a matter for complicated theorizing. It is a matter of common sense. There is no denying that our happiness is inextricably bound up with the happiness of others. There is no denying that if society suffers, we ourselves suffer. Nor is there any denying that the more our hearts and minds are afflicted with ill-will, the more miserable we become.[19]

The practice of compassion enhances well-being and happiness. Neuroscience and the study of human physiology also confirm that it is good medicine.[20]

Throughout our story, Vicky illustrates compassion. Her behaviors are consistently rooted in honesty, kindness, and respect: meeting others where they are, moving closer to engage, delaying negative judgments, and inflicting no harm. She assumes the best in others until consistent data confirms otherwise—and even then, responds first by changing how she relates to them so as to try another way to bring out their best. Nowhere is Vicky's practice of compassion more tested than in her dealings with Michael.

Practicing compassion may require training in learning to say *no* with clarity and *yes* more often. That may seem counterintuitive advice, yet it is not. *No* is the word we use to protect ourselves and to stand up for all that matters to us. It can anger others and destroy relationships, so we often say *yes* when we really want to say *no,* or say *no* poorly, or say nothing at all. Learning to deliver a clear yet positive *no,* according to negotiating coach William Ury,[21] fosters the honest communication and authenticity at the heart of strong relationships. The comedy world of improvisation reminds us that *yes, and*[22] is a way to validate and build on what others have initiated and explore new alternatives—foundational strengths in teamwork.

Try This

Research shows that compassion skills can be developed. Like any skilled behavior, you need instruction in *how to* and a commitment to practice. Compassion includes four basic steps: (1) recognize suffering in others, (2) acknowledge it, (3) set an intention to do something, and (4) take an action. Dr. Amit Sood lays out a plan for how to practice compassion.[23] Choose a step, and see how using it over a period of time improves the quality of life for you and for others. Go slow to avoid compassion fatigue![24] You must gradually build up your capabilities to stand with, but not take in, others' emotions.

1. Look at difficult behaviors in others as a call for help. Respond with kindness.

2. Delay snap and negative judgments: try to walk in others' shoes and acknowledge the urgency that must be driving some important unmet need for them.

3. Remember that no one intentionally sets out to suffer or behave ineffectively.

4. See yourself in others' mistakes: the journey they travel today is one you may have traveled before or will in the future.

5. Pay it forward: perform random acts of kindness; do something good and forget it!

6. Act with humility: act to help, not wow!

7. Recognize the difference between fear and caution: caution is rational; fear shackles.

8. Move toward others: lean in in simple ways.

███████

UNHOOK

Reflection and Journaling

Donald Schön describes reflection as "a dialogue of thinking and doing through which I become more skillful."[25] It is a process of looking inside to learn more about yourself and your relationship to something that matters. Journaling—taking notes on your reflections—aids that process. The goal is to get clearer about what's going on inside you, and how that influences your take on the situation.

> It is necessary to sit on a rock and ask,
> Who am I, where have I been, and where am I going?
> —*Carl Sandburg*

In reflecting on a difficult relationship, a good way to begin is to ask yourself, What story am I telling myself about what's happening with this other person? What kind of person do I think he or she is? What do I believe the other person is doing to me, and why?

You can then move on to deeper questions like, What feelings does this other person trigger in me? Can I think of other situations or people who have caused me to feel the same way? What do my feelings and reactions cause me to do when I'm with this person? How well do my actions work? Can I identify old patterns of behavior that this person may be triggering? In constructing your story, heed Schön's advice to allow yourself to "experience surprise, puzzlement, or confusion."[26] Difficult relationships are messy, and you can learn better if you're willing to engage the mess.

Once you've written your story about the other person and yourself, you can step back and reflect on what you see. Is it the only story you could tell? What other ways to think about this situation might work better? Could a different take free you to respond differently? If reflection of this nature is something you've rarely done, it may seem awkward and difficult at first. You may wonder if the benefits justify the time it takes. If you keep at it, it can help you recognize and unhook from feelings and perceptions that lock you into unproductive patterns. The ultimate goal is creative freedom—seeing new and better options for dealing with a difficult relationship.

An added benefit to reflection and journaling is the potential for personal healing. Healing is a shift in perspective.[27] This can come when you understand the stories you tell yourself and see their impact on your life over time. Difficult people trigger emotions and the reliving of painful experiences that remain unresolved for you. Many have testified to the healing power in writing difficult experiences down.[28] It is "a very sturdy ladder out of the pit" for Alice Walker, author of *The Color Purple*.[29] For Ray Bradbury, it is life's ballast:

> If I let a day go by without writing, I grow uneasy. Two days and I am in tremor. Three and I suspect lunacy. Four and I might as well be a hog, suffering the flux in a wallow. An hour's writing is tonic. I'm on my feet, running in circles, and yelling for a clean pair of spats.[30]

Journaling takes no innate talents, although you'll become better at it with experience. Remember, you write for only one audience, you. And have patience! Penetrating the familiar to see its deeper meaning is hard work.[31]

Try This

You can build self-reflection into your life in simple ways. If journaling seems too daunting at first, find other ways to develop the habit of writing down experiences to aid your personal and professional growth. Start slowly and see how it goes. You might try:

1. Set aside five minutes at the end of the day for you to write down a sentence or two on what troubled you today and what delighted you. Use your computer or write in longhand in a bedside notebook. Look for themes and trends over time.

2. Keep a gratitude jar with a pencil and small slips of paper beside it. Each morning, think of one thing you are grateful for. Write it on a piece of paper and drop it in the jar. Variations on this might include, for example, writing your top goal for the day. Or write in the evening, and record the moment in the day when you were most proud of your actions. Have fun!

Consulting: Solicit Input, Seek Support, Find a Good Sounding Board

Unhooking requires letting go of whatever is keeping you stuck. A friend or coach can make that easier. Look for support and counsel from others whom you can depend on to provide good input and to help you stay balanced. It can be formal or informal, paid or not paid. It's easy to feel alone and confused when you are struggling to handle a difficult relationship. It helps to have someone to talk to about the challenges and possible options.

> There are times to stay put and what you want will come to you, and there are times to go out into the world and find such a thing for yourself.[32]
>
> — *Lemony Snicket*

The ideal consultant is someone you trust, who asks good questions, who has broad and relevant experience, who can engage you to think more broadly about the issues, and who can be objective about the challenges you face. Not all consultants are created equal, nor do they bring the same value. You enhance your skills in using consultants well when you:

Choose wisely. Vicky made a good choice in turning to her former boss, Peter. Vicky trusts Peter. He knows her skills, limits, and experiences from their past work together, and he has already demonstrated a commitment to her professional development. Peter's position in the organization gives him the added benefit of a grounded understanding of Vicky's challenges and of key players like Michael. In choosing a consultant, ask yourself:

- Who can I trust?
- Who can help me learn?
- Who brings relevant skills and experiences for the situation I face?

Know what you want. Choosing the right consultant also involves knowing what you want. You'll be frustrated if you seek a shoulder to cry on and get someone who wants to solve your technical problems. Vicky knew how to use Peter as a sounding board and support through their periodic telephone calls. She also consulted with Michael on things he knew, like office personnel. She got Carlos the technical help he needed to advance the operations. In choosing a consultant, ask yourself:

- What role do I want a consultant to play? (Am I looking for technical input? Personal support and coaching? A sounding board? An extra set of eyes? Some combination of all of these?)
- How will we work together? (Do I want face-to-face meetings? Periodic telephone check-ins? A report outlining findings and suggestions? Something else?)

Communicate your needs. Vicky wanted periodic telephone check-ins with Peter, and she confirmed his willingness to play that role. Getting what you want from a consultant means proactive management of the relationship and a willingness to communicate your needs clearly and directly. In working with a consultant, ask yourself:

- What kind of agreement—formal or informal—do I need to assure the other knows what I want and need?
- How will we periodically take stock on whether things are working as planned?

Use your consultant effectively. Vicky made particularly good use of her conversations with Peter to test her thinking, seek new ideas, and build confidence. She was direct, honest, and to the point. She was also willing to ask when she wanted more, as in her request for Peter's casual call to Michael. In working with a consultant, ask yourself:

- How well is this relationship expanding my capacities to understand myself, others, the situation, and my options? What needs to happen to make it better?
- How well is this relationship expanding my learning? What needs to happen to make it better?

Try This

Use the questions provided in this section to determine the kind of support and help you need from others. How will you arrange to get it—and to assess periodically if it is meeting your needs? Managing

(continued)

(*continued*)
difficult people is stressful, and may make you heavy company. Forewarn unpaid consultants and friends, and check in regularly with them to maintain those important relationships. Support is essential in managing difficult people situations. Cases involving workplace bullying are extremely stressful, difficult, and complex. These should not be handled alone or with others who lack strong knowledge of the dangerous and destructive dynamics.[33]

Mindful Vigilance

The Buddha said, "Mindfulness is the direct path to freedom." You can see why this is so in Ellen Langer's description of mindfulness as revolving around "psychological states that are really different versions of the same thing: (1) openness to novelty; (2) alertness to distinction; (3) sensitivity to different contexts; (4) implicit, if not explicit, awareness of multiple perspectives; and (5) orientation in the present."[35] These all point to mindfulness as flexible and receptive awareness—a process of reflecting on what's going on around you and inside you. Vicky is a model of this. Langer concludes that the "grooves of mindlessness run deep"[36] in too many people.

> By mindfully considering data not as stable commodities, but as sources of ambiguity, we become more observant.[34]
>
> —*Ellen J. Langer*

Langer distinguishes between hypervigilance and soft vigilance.[37] In hypervigilance, you focus intently on something important or threatening to you. Hypervigilance is not always a bad thing, especially in the face of real danger. It's energizing, but tiring. Mindfulness can help you achieve soft vigilance—a calm and confident awareness of what's important to you and where you need to focus your attention. Not every bump in the road is a major threat or sign of impending doom. You'll burn out quickly if you approach them as if they were.

There are different types of meditation and each provides a path to practice mindfulness.[38] So do journaling, self-reflection activities, prayer, deep breathing, guided-relaxation exercises, playing a musical instrument, walking a labyrinth (or tracing a pattern with your hand), deliberate practice of the virtues (gratitude, acceptance, kindness, forgiveness, compassion, joy), knitting, walks in nature, appreciating art, immersing yourself in a good book—any activity that counters the mind's predisposition to wander and returns it to a focus on the here and now. Find what works for you! Pay attention.

Try This

Experiment with various activities. You can, for example:

1. *Practice a simple breathing meditation:* Find a place to sit comfortably, relax, and focus on your breathing—the flow of air in and out of your nostrils. Initially, you may find that your mind is flooded with distracting thoughts, but keep returning to a focus on your breathing.

2. *Use a book of written reflections:* Set aside time to read and think about one each day.

3. *Designate a virtue:* Choose a virtue and find opportunities in the course of the day to act upon it. Make Monday, for example, a day of gratitude and deliberately seek opportunities to identify simple things or people you are grateful for. Think about them and wish them well. Dedicate your good work that day to them.

Enhancing Resilience, Building Mental Strength

There is a large literature on building resilience. The American Psychological Association's Resilience Campaign[40] is a good starting point for identifying resources and helpful actions. The APA suggests 10 basic practices:

> Human beings have enormous resilience.[39]
> —*Muhammad Yunus*

1. Make strong connections with family and friends: everyone needs their tribe!

2. Avoid seeing crises as insurmountable: it's easy to lose perspective in times of strain.

3. Accept change as part of living: change happens!

4. Set goals and do something regularly to achieve them: small accomplishments matter.

5. Take action rather than wishing problems would go away: personal agency feels good.

6. Find opportunities to learn and grow: you'll discover things of which to be proud.

7. Nurture a positive view of yourself: celebrate your strengths.

8. Keep things in perspective: s___ happens!

9. Aim for a hopeful outlook: find good things in your life—savor them!

10. Take care of yourself: engage in activities you love!

Readers may find that many of the habits and practices discussed in this section of the book strengthen their resilience—activities such as journaling, practicing the virtues, embracing compassion, generating options, constructing scenarios, embracing joy, and meditation.

In another book that we coauthored,[41] we proposed strategies to sustain leadership vitality and resolve. Those involve attention to five key areas—we called them the 5 B's:

1. Managing **boundaries** between oneself and others, between your life and your work.

2. Attending to our **body** in ways to maintain basic good health.

3. Bringing **balance** among work, friends and family, and leisure.

4. Finding activities that feed the soul, like the **beauty** and recuperative power of the arts and nature.

5. Increasing the odds that you'll **bounce** back from stress and challenge through resilience training.

Building resilience is facilitated by adding goals and practices like those suggested here. Psychotherapist Amy Morin cautions that best intentions are often derailed not by the goals you set for yourself in the face of adversity and stress, but rather the tacit habits of the mind that block your ability to achieve them. She identifies dysfunctional habits you may need to let go of so as to stay mentally strong:[42]

1. Don't waste time feeling sorry for yourself.
2. Don't give away your power.
3. Don't shy away from change.
4. Don't waste time on things you can't change.
5. Don't worry about pleasing people.
6. Don't fear calculated risks.
7. Don't dwell on the past.
8. Don't make the same mistakes again and again.
9. Don't resent others' success.
10. Don't give up in the face of failure.
11. Don't fear time alone.
12. Don't feel the world owes you anything.
13. Don't expect results immediately.

Try This

The APA and Bolman and Gallos lists offer approaches for building your capabilities to thrive in the face of difficult situations. Review the lists. Where are you strong? Which areas and practices need shoring up? Make an action plan for growing supports and habits you need for your long-term success. Amy Morin identifies beliefs and behaviors that can hold you back. Which are you holding on to, and what is your plan for jettisoning them—one by one?

Joyful Attention Training

You have undoubtedly experienced moments of "flow"[44]—when you felt "in the zone" and so deeply engaged in an activity that the world

> Find a place inside where there's joy, and the joy will burn out the pain.[43]
> —*Joseph Campbell*

around you disappeared. Time seems to fly. Professional musicians aim for this in their performances;[45] and NBA coaching great, Phil Jackson, designed his coaching strategy around helping his players get there.[46] But you don't need to be a professional athlete or musician to intentionally train and direct your mind to be more focused and relaxed. How can you develop habits of the mind that underpin the kind of calm, focused, and nonjudgmental persistence that Vicky brought to her work? Sound complicated? It really isn't. Your attention is like a muscle. Work it with regular mental exercises to make it stronger. A bit of neuroscience explains why and how.[47]

The mind is never at rest. The idling brain is as active when you are "vegging out" as when doing a crossword puzzle! Unless you direct it, your brain will do what comes naturally: neurons will fire spontaneously with thoughts about *you*—your problems, woes, and *what ifs* of life, spinning internal dialogues and stories that randomly weave together your past, present, and future. The idling mind is a wandering mind, easily distracted by things other than what you are doing or wanting to think about.[48]

Three things about this are important for our discussion here. One, it is as important to be able to turn off parts of your brain as to turn on others. Two, you can turn off dysfunctional ruminations by choosing to engage in an externally oriented, goal-directed task. Three, what helps you refocus your attention in the short term retrains your brain over time. Neurons that fire together stay together, hardwiring your brain.[49] You want habits that "right-wire" it. That's the joy in attention training.

Dr. Amit Sood offers strategies for retraining your attention, and suggests practicing four to eight times a day during your training period. You may have to undo lifelong cognitive tendencies, and "just as a river needs time to carve a canyon, resilient new brain pathways depend on repetitive and deeply felt experiences."[50] The activities ask you to notice and enjoy more deeply, connect your thoughts and senses, look for novelty in the everyday, and suspend judgment. Many take but a few minutes to practice, and they bring increased pleasure and joy.

Try This

We suggest a few personal favorites from Dr. Sood's training to get you started. Enjoy as you experiment and grow!

1. *Find novelty in a relationship:* greet another as if meeting after a long time; devote time to sharing something new or newly rediscovered for each of you.

2. *Find the extraordinary in the ordinary:* pay attention to some detail around you in a new way—the blue of the sky today, the different shades of green in the grass, the pattern in the rug you have walked mindlessly on so many times before. Let a new discovery of beauty or novelty wash over you!

3. *Start your day with gratitude:* use it to turn off the stress in waking up to your usual *to do* and *dread* lists.

4. *End your day with gratitude:* remind yourself of something wonderful!

5. *Notice nature:* as the Buddhist adage goes: spend 10 minutes each day quietly in nature. If you are very busy and overloaded, spend 20 minutes.

6. *Smile more, frown less:* Your brain doesn't know you are faking it, and a smile releases beneficial endorphins!

7. *Eat or exercise mindfully:* pay attention to time, place, pace, posture, and other sensory experiences. And mindful eating is a good way to control weight!

8. *Try small random acts of kindness:* kind attention is externally focused attention, and kindness toward others boosts your mood.

9. *Find something in another to be impressed by:* the Hindi word *namaste* means the divine in me salutes the divine in you. See the divine in those around you. Namaste!

REVISE THE SCRIPT

Generating Options

Chris Argyris uses the term "skilled incompetence" to describe well-learned behaviors that you perform automatically and without thinking even though they don't produce the results you want. Personal change requires interrupting automatic patterns that aren't working. A good way to begin is to ask two questions:

> We must reinvent a future free of blinders so that we can choose from real options.[51]
>
> —*David Suzuki*

1. What other options should I consider?
2. If I were at my best, what would I do?

Brainstorm until you have multiple options. Enlist a friend or coach to help you increase the possibilities. Once you have a promising choice, write out a script just as if you were writing a play. What would you say? What would the other person say? How would you respond? Play it out back and forth. Keep polishing until you have a script that leads to a good ending.

Then, script in hand, practice. Professional musicians practice for hours so that muscle memory carries them through moments of stage fright or forgetfulness and builds their confidence. As you rehearse different responses, you increase your repertoire of options and make success more likely. There's no guarantee that a new script will work as well in the heat of action as in your imagination, but practice and preparation improve your odds.

Suppose, for example, you have a colleague who regularly finds fault with you for things you did or didn't do. The criticism annoys you every time, and you usually respond with something that makes things worse. Here's an example:

Other: [Sounding frustrated and annoyed.] How come you never answered my e-mail? I sent it more than an hour ago. You know how important this project is, and you're holding everything up. How can you be so irresponsible?

You: [Annoyed by Other's tone and furious at being called "irresponsible."] You think I don't know how important this project is? You think I don't have anything to do but respond to your e-mails? Clean up your own act and get off my case!

Annoyance is a legitimate feeling, but an angry attack almost guarantees the conversation will go downhill. What other script could you write for yourself? One option would be to ignore the personal criticism and focus on the task. For example, you might ask a simple question like, "What do we need to do now?" You could reflect Other's comment back: "You think not getting back in an hour was irresponsible?" You could gently confront, "Irresponsible feels unfair when we're both working as hard as we can." Or confront less gently: "Do you think blaming me will move the project along faster?" You can probably think of other possibilities.

There is never a single right answer, and there are always options. Look for something that lets you script yourself as a calm and confident professional, so that you can control your feelings rather than let them control you. You also want something that breaks the pattern by responding in a way that your difficult person isn't expecting. Vicky offers multiple examples in her exchanges with Michael and her team members—take another look at the story to review them and what they accomplished. Surprise can interrupt another's unproductive script and open an opportunity for a more productive conversation.

The process of generating and rehearsing options is most likely to work when you do it offline, away from the troublesome person or situation, and when you have time to engage in creative thinking. Once you've generated options, you can focus on those that seem most promising, develop scripts for yourself, and practice how you could employ them.

Try This

Prepare for your next meeting with your difficult person using the preceding recommendations to generate options and write a new

(continued)

(*continued*)

script for your next interaction. Preparation brings comfort—and reduces the stress difficult people generate for you. It also encourages your flexibility and broadens your repertoire of interpersonal strategies.

Creating Scenarios

In dealing with difficult people, it is often hard to predict how the other person will respond. But because it's hard doesn't mean that we shouldn't try. A powerful way to clarify thinking and to test assumptions is to develop scenarios or stories about how specific choices might play out over time. Scenario building has been used in industry for a long time—a way to "rehearse the future" and anticipate the impact of a host of unpredictable forces and choices.

> If you want something new, you have to stop doing something old.
> — *Peter F. Drucker*

There's plenty of advice out there on how to build scenarios if you want a more structured method: strategic planners approach it as though it were a science.[52] Or this can be a more informal and playful process of looking ahead.[53] Our goal here is to encourage you to get used to crafting alternative stories for yourself about possible futures based on different choices and different sets of assumptions. Your creative scenarios may identify interesting plot twists, powerful constituents to inform or involve, unpredictable environmental factors, winners, and losers—things you'd want to know in advance of facing them at work!

An oil company, for example, would make different decisions if it knew that the price of oil was going up rather than down. But oil companies have learned that the price of oil is fiendishly difficult to predict. One way to deal with that uncertainty is to develop alternative scenarios. Suppose that the price is going up over the next five years. What kind of world would you be in? What choices would you make? How would each affect the kind of future you want to create? Now make the opposite assumption. If the price is sure to go down, what will the world look like? What would you do in that world?

You can use the same process in thinking about your difficult relationship. Suppose, for example, that you're wondering how you could talk to a person with whom you are having great difficulty or who is as unpredictable as Michael is for Vicky. As you think about how it might go, imagine three distinct ways the other might respond: (1) receptively, (2) angrily, and (3) by withdrawing and going behind your back to get even with you—or any other set of alternatives that seem helpful to try. Develop a scenario around each of those three possibilities, asking yourself how you would approach the other person in each case. What would you do with someone who's receptive? Someone who's angry? Someone who might go behind your back? Then ask if you can develop a robust approach for yourself that has a good chance of working across the different possible futures.

Try This

Look for a win-win by thinking through and creating multiple scenarios in advance of your next meeting with your difficult other. Equally important, reflect on your comfort or discomfort in using any one of them for insights into your triggers or to anticipate any unhelpful responses. Think about asking someone to role-play these with you, and fine-tune what you learn to increase the odds of relationship progress and learning from the real exchange.

Humor

There is ample evidence of the health and professional benefits of laughter and humor. Neuroscience has shown that humor embodies

> Wear life loosely.[54]
> —*Bernie S. Siegel*

many of the creative right brain's most powerful attributes— understanding situations in context, getting the big picture, and combining different elements in new alignments. The effective use of humor can be an accurate marker of managerial effectiveness, emotional intelligence, and innovation.[55] Humor plays a number of important roles at work: it expresses skepticism, reduces hostility, relieves tension, helps communicate difficult messages, and lessens status differences.[56] Above all, it is a way to illuminate and break frame, indicating that any single definition of a situation is arbitrary and open for deeper investigation.[57] Stanford professor emeritus Jim

March suggests guidelines for encouraging productive playfulness in organizations: treat goals as hypotheses, intuition as real, hypocrisy as transition, memory as an enemy, and experience as a theory.[58]

Humor encourages you to wear life loosely, and that is especially important in situations involving difficult people. Vicky and Peter regularly punctuated their conversations with humor—putting Vicky's concerns in perspective, bringing a more relaxed tone to their joint problem solving, and strengthening their enjoyment of the mentor relationship and each other. Laughter cushions the most stressful bumps in life and enhances your connections to others and your physical well-being: it releases the pain-reducing, relaxation-promoting chemicals called endorphins and the bonding hormone called oxytocin.[59]

Try This

Find ways to laugh more, and set goals to laugh more every day. It's that simple! Daniel Pink[60] suggests a portfolio of activities, including videos and meetings at one of the growing number of international Laughter Clubs, based on Dr. Madan Kataria's laughter yoga.[61] You will know what tickles your fancy: humor books, movies, improvisation games, comedy tapes, time with witty friends. Laughing more will also remind you to take yourself less seriously, and you'll be better prepared to face your difficult challenges.

ENGAGE—EVOLVE OR EXIT

Skilled Candor

Skilled candor is the ability to say what you know, think, feel, or want in a way that others can get your message. It's a vital skill for communication, leadership, and persuasion. Skilled candor is not venting, bluster, argumentativeness, or attack, which prime others to resist rather than understand you.

> Never ignore the elephant in the room. That's rude. Play with it and introduce it.
>
> —*Donna Lynn Hope*

It begins with a willingness to tell the truth and share your reality with others. This sometimes takes courage because you expect a negative reaction to what you have to say. An example is naming the "elephant in the room"—the uncomfortable topic that everyone is aware of but afraid to talk about. Some of the most powerful examples of advocacy involve the willingness to express uncomfortable truths. At other times, candor involves expressing uncertainty or lack of clarity as a way of engaging others in exploration.

Skilled candor requires the ability to communicate messages so that other people can hear and understand them. This is especially important in situations in which difficult others may feel threatened or embarrassed.[62] One such communication skill is the ability to position facts and feelings in a larger story—a bigger picture that frames your thoughts in a way that gives them meaning and coherence. Another specific form of skilled candor is effective feedback, which we discuss in the next section. Person-centered negotiating techniques[63] suggest helpful strategies such as separating the person from the problem, focusing on mutual interests and gains, and using objective data. Warmth, grace, and a calm voice are assets. Vicky offers multiple examples of calm yet assertive leadership. Practice yours!

It helps to clearly understand your motivation and thinking about difficult others—especially any private explanations of their actions or attributions of motivation that you may hold. As Vicky shows, know thyself and suspend judgments to increase your impact.

Try This

Chris Argyris introduced a technique called the double-sided case. You may want to use it to learn from an exchange that did not go well—or anticipate one that raises your concern. Write out the case in the format described further on. Once done, spend time thinking about it using the questions provided. After having done that, find someone to discuss the case with you. Give them a copy. We are all

(continued)

(*continued*)

blind to behaviors that others may see clearly. Get an outside perspective on your actions!

1. Choose an exchange with another that you found challenging or anticipate will be.

2. In a paragraph or two, write out your goal for the meeting (that is, what you wanted or hoped to accomplish).

3. Then, take a sheet of paper and write out a brief portion of the actual dialogue as you remember (or anticipate) it, using the following format.

Your underlying thoughts and feelings	What was said:
	Me:
	Other:
	Me:
	Other:
	and so forth

1. In the right-hand column, write out what you recall was actually said or anticipate might be said (that is, what did/will you say? and what did/will Other respond?).

2. In the left-hand column, put down any thoughts or feelings that you had or might have in the course of the conversation that were not expressed.

3. After you have written all of this out, study your case and see what you notice. Questions to reflect on might include:

   a. What did you say?

   b. How did the other respond?

   c. Why do you think he or she did?

   d. What were you thinking or feeling that you did not say?

e. Why did you choose not discuss these? What did you anticipate would happen if you did?

f. How well did you accomplish your goals for the exchange?

g. What could you have done differently for a different (or better)
outcome?

Giving and Receiving Good Feedback

Feedback is information that helps you understand the impact of your actions. It is essential when you're trying to gauge how others perceive and respond to what you do. The challenge in both getting and giving

> Feedback is the breakfast—and the lunch, dinner, and midnight snack—of champions.[64]
> —*Ken Blanchard*

feedback is to convey information that the receiver can hear and use. Usable feedback is **descriptive** and **specific** rather than evaluative and vague. "You did a lousy job," for example, is unhelpful because it evaluates rather than describes, and doesn't specify what the other person did that was "lousy." If, for example, another person gave a presentation that was confusing and lacked a message that was clear to you, you could say, "I had trouble following your line of thinking. It would have helped me if you made a clearer statement at the end to summarize your main points." This makes it clear that you are **describing your reaction**—it wasn't clear to you, though it might have been clear to someone else. It also describes a way that a particular part of the presentation might have been modified. Descriptive and specific feedback is easier for the recipient to both hear and to test. Asking someone else, "Did you feel my presentation was lousy?" probably will not elicit a helpful response. But asking, "Did you feel the presentation needed a better summary at the end?" would help test whether others felt that that was an issue.

Good feedback is also **timely:** we are all more motivated to listen and learn if we are receiving others' reactions close to the event. It also helps if feedback is offered to **support learning** rather than to punish or zap another. Feedback is a gift offered so that others may choose to learn about their impact.

Try This

Look at some of the many online resources available about giving good feedback. Ken Blanchard has a particularly good one on his professional website.[65] Use your new insights to practice improving your skills. Write out a script. Discuss it with others.

NOTES

PREFACE

1. Lee G. Bolman and Joan V. Gallos, *Reframing Academic Leadership* (San Francisco: Jossey-Bass, 2011), chapter 10.
2. Michael Maccoby, *Narcissistic Leaders: Who Succeeds and Who Fails* (Boston: Harvard Business School Press, 2007).

INTRODUCTION

1. Samuel Taylor Coleridge, *The Rime of the Ancient Mariner* (The Poetry Foundation, 1834). www.poetryfoundation.org/poem/173253. Accessed October 4, 2015.
2. Michael Housman and Dylan Minor, *Toxic Workers* (HBS working paper 16–057, November 2015) (Boston: Harvard Business School, 2015). The authors studied more than 50,000 workers across 11 different firms and concluded that toxic workers are expensive and destructive. Their impact runs the gamut from potential legal or regulatory costs for a company to more local impact, such as declining unit and organizational morale, damage to a firm's reputation, and driving others to leave the organization faster and more frequently, thereby increasing training and turnover costs, and loss of vital institutional history and experience.
3. Harry Stack Sullivan, *The Interpersonal Theory of Psychiatry* (New York: Norton, 1953).

4. Matthew A. Killingsworth and Daniel T. Gilbert, "A Wandering Mind Is an Unhappy Mind," *Science* 330, no. 6006 (November 12, 2010): 932. [DOI:10.1126/science.1192439].

5. Randy L. Bucknew, "The Serendipitous Discovery of the Brain's Default Network," *Neuroimage* 62 (2012): 11–37.

6. Amit Sood, *The Mayo Clinic Guide to Stress-Free Living* (Philadelphia: Da Capo Press, 2013), 2–12. Sood distinguishes ruminations (repetitive, undirected thoughts about the past that trigger stress and negative emotions) from worries (similar, unhelpful, and automatic thoughts about the future). Both predispose the brain to depression, and depression makes it harder to stop further ruminations and worries or to engage in productive and adaptive thinking.

7. Amy Morin, *13 Things Mentally Strong People Do: Take Back Your Power, Embrace Change, Face Your Fears, and Train Your Brain for Happiness and Success* (New York: HarperCollins, 2014).

8. Katherine Crowley and Kathi Elster, *Working with You Is Killing Me* (New York: Warner Business Books, 2006). A summary version of the authors' model is available at http://abcnews.go.com/GMA/Books/story?id=1796805&page=1.

9. Robert Sutton, *The No Asshole Rule: Building a Civilized Workplace and Surviving One That Isn't* (New York: Business Plus/Hachette Book Group, 2010).

INTERLUDE 1. COPING WITH BULLIES

1. There is a large and growing literature on bullying in the workplace. Of particular note: John Lipinski and Laura M. Crothers, *Bullying in the Workplace: Causes, Symptoms, and Remedies* (London: Routledge, 2013); Jaime Lester, *Workplace Bullying in Higher Education* (London: Routledge, 2013); Gary Namie and Ruth F. Namie, *The Bully-Free Workplace: Stop Jerks, Weasels, and Snakes from Killing Your Organization* (Hoboken, NJ: John Wiley & Sons, 2011); Gary Namie and Ruth F. Namie, *The Bully at Work: What You Can Do to Stop the Hurt and Reclaim Your Dignity on the Job*, 2nd ed. (Naperville, IL: Sourcebooks, Inc., 2009); and Darla J. Twale and Barbara M. De Luca, *Faculty Incivility: The Rise of the Academic Bully Culture and What to Do about It* (Hoboken, NJ: John Wiley & Sons, 2008). Books exploring the

phenomenon as a process of scapegoating include: John M. Dyckman and Joseph A. Cutler, *Scapegoats at Work: Taking the Bull's-Eye off Your Back* (Westport, CT: Praeger, 2003).

2. www.workplacebullying.org/individuals/problem/who-gets-targeted.

3. Joan Borysenko, *Minding the Body, Mending the Mind* (New York: Bantam Books, 1988).

4. www.workplacebullying.org/individuals/problem/definition.

5. Dr. Herbert Benson developed a deep breathing technique in the 1970s called *The Relaxation Response* as a way to counter the body's autonomic reaction to stress in the face of real or perceived dangers and that can lead to health concerns such as high blood pressure, suppressed immune system responses, increased susceptibility to colds and other illnesses, anxiety, and depression. A revised version of Benson's best-selling classic is Herbert Benson (with Miriam Klipper), *The Relaxation Response* (New York: HarperTorch, 2000). An abbreviated version of his technique is available at www.health.harvard.edu/mind-and-mood/relaxation-techniques-breath-control-helps-quell-errant-stress-response.

6. Daniel Goleman, *Emotional Intelligence: Why It Can Matter More than IQ* (New York: Bantam Dell, 2005).

INTERLUDE 2. MANAGING THE BOSS

1. Grumpy or cantankerous behavior under pressure is different from antisocial pathologies that express themselves in workplace bullying. Bullies are threatened by the competence of others, and their behaviors are driven by deep internal inadequacies and psychological causes. To understand the differences, see Dr. Jane McGregor and Tim McGregor, *The Empathy Trap: Understanding Antisocial Personalities* (London: Sheldon Press, 2013).

2. Books of note on the topic include: Aryanne Oade, *Free Yourself from Workplace Bullying: Become Bully-Proof and Regain Control of Your Life* (Oxford, UK: Mint Hall Publishing, 2015); John Hoover, *How to Work for an Idiot: Survive and Thrive without Killing Your Boss*, 2nd ed. (Pompton Plains, NJ: The Career Press, 2011); Robert Sutton, *Good Boss, Bad Boss: How to Be the Best and Learn from the Worst* (New York: Hachette Books, 2010); Katherine Crowley and Kathi Elster, *Working for You Isn't Working for Me: How to Get Ahead When Your*

Boss Holds You Back (New York: Penguin Press, 2009); Lynn Taylor, *Tame Your Terrible Office Tyrant: How to Manage Childish Boss Behavior and Thrive in Your Job* (Hoboken, NJ: John Wiley & Sons, 2009); Gini Graham Scott, *A Survival Guide for Working with Bad Bosses: Dealing with Bullies, Idiots, Backstabbers, and other Managers from Hell* (New York: AMACOM, 2006); Barbara Kellerman, *Bad Leadership: What It Is, How It Happens, Why It Matters* (Boston: Harvard Business School Press, 2004); Harry Chambers, *My Way or the Highway: The Micromanagement Survival Guide* (San Francisco: Berrette-Koehler, 2004).

3. Barbara Kellerman, *Bad Leadership: What It Is, How It Happens, Why It Matters* (Boston: Harvard Business School Press, 2004), chapter 4–10.
4. www.workplacebullying.org/individuals/problem/definition.
5. See   www.workplacebullying.org/individuals/problem/who-gets-targeted or http://bullyonline.org/workbully/amibeing.htm#what_triggers_bullying.

INTERLUDE 3. LEARNING WITH TENACITY

1. Joan V. Gallos, ed., *Business Leadership* (San Francisco: Jossey-Bass/John Wiley & Sons, 2008), chapter 13 ("Making Sense of Organizations: Leadership, Frames, and Everyday Theories of the Situation").
2. Robert Bramson, *Coping with Difficult People: The Proven-Effective Battle Plan That Has Helped Millions Deal with the Troublemakers in Their Lives at Home and at Work* (New York: Dell, 1988), chapter 9.

INTERLUDE 4. LEADING WITH PURPOSE

1. Warren Bennis and Robert J. Thomas, "Resilience and the Crucibles of Leadership," in Joan V. Gallos, ed., *Business Leadership* (San Francisco: Jossey-Bass/John Wiley & Sons, 2008), chapter 39. A version of this chapter is accessible at the *Harvard Business Review* website, accessed December 2, 2015 at https://hbr.org/2002/09/crucibles-of-leadership.
2. Niccolo Machiavelli, *The Prince,* Project Gutenberg e-version (W. K. Marriott, Translator, 2012), www.gutenberg.org/files/1232/1232-h/1232-h.htm.

3. In his classic book, organizational psychologist Barry Oshry provides a helpful understanding of system dynamics and the reasons for our blindness to them. He identifies the human tendency for people to see only what is around them (spatial blindness) and to ignore much of the past (temporal blindness). See Barry Oshry, *Seeing Systems: Unlocking the Mysteries of Organizational Life* (San Francisco: Berrett-Koehler, 1995); Michael Sales, "Leadership and the Power of Position: Understanding Structural Dynamics in Everyday Organizational Life," in Joan V. Gallos, ed., *Business Leadership* (San Francisco: Jossey-Bass/John Wiley & Sons, 2008, chapter 14 builds on Oshry's work and illustrates how and why organizational roles elicit predictable behaviors. Bolman and Deal have created a classroom simulation based on Oshry's work, and can elicit predictable behaviors based on one's role and level in the hierarchy. See Lee G. Bolman and Terrence E. Deal, "A Simple but Powerful Power Simulation," *Exchange: The Organizational Behavior Teaching Review* IV, no. 3 (Summer 1979): 38–41, www. leebolman.com/Teaching%20materials/B%20&%20D%20Exchange% 20Power%20Simulation%202%20Column.pdf.

4. Lee G. Bolman and Terrence E. Deal, *Reframing Organizations: Artistry, Choice and Leadership*, 4th ed. (San Francisco: Jossey-Bass/John Wiley & Sons, 2008), chapter 2 (23–40).

5. Research on individual-organizational fit across cultures provides interesting insights. See, for example, I. S. Oh, R. P. Guay, K. Kim, C. M. Harold, J. H. Lee, C. G. Heo, and K. H. Shin, "Fit Happens Globally: A Meta-Analytic Comparison of the Relationships of Person-Environment Fit Dimensions with Work Attitudes and Performance Across East Asia, Europe, and North America," *Personnel Psychology* 67, no. 1 (2014): 99–152. Popular press reviews of research trends include Sylvia Ann Hewlett, "Asians in America: What's Holding Back the 'Model Minority?'" *Forbes Woman Online,* July 28, 2011, www.forbes.com/ sites/sylviaannhewlett/2011/07/28/asians-in-america-whats-holding-back-the-model-minority.

6. Amy Morin, *13 Things Mentally Strong People Don't Do: Take Back Your Power, Embrace Change, Face Your Fears, and Train Your Brain for Happiness and Success* (New York: William Morrow, 2014).

7. A more detailed discussion of strategies to sustain the leader by the authors includes: Lee G. Bolman and Joan V. Gallos, *Reframing Academic Leadership* (San Francisco: Jossey-Bass, 2011), chapters 12 and 13;

and Joan V. Gallos, "Learning from the Toxic Trenches: The Winding Road to Healthier Organizations—and to Healthy Everyday Leaders," *Journal of Management Inquiry* 17, no. 4 (December 2008): 354–367. In addition, Part Five (Sustaining the Leader) in Joan V. Gallos, ed., *Business Leadership* (San Francisco: Jossey-Bass/John Wiley & Sons, 2008) contains six chapters on this important set of issues: chapter 35, "A Survival Guide for Leaders" (by Ronald A. Heifetz and Marty Linsky), chapter 36, "Preserving Integrity, Profitability, and Soul" (by David Batstone), chapter 37, "Learning for Leadership: Failure as a Second Chance" (by David L. Dotich, James L. Noel, and Norman Walker), chapter 38, "Nourishing the Soul of the Leader: Inner Growth Matters" (by Andre L. Delbecq), chapter 39, "Resilience and the Crucibles of Leadership" (by Warren G. Bennis and Robert J. Thomas), and chapter 40, "Choose Hope: On Creating a Hopeful Future" (by Andrew Razeghi).

CHAPTER 15. A WARNING FROM MICHAEL

1. Warren Bennis, *On Becoming a Leader* (New York: Basic Books, 2003), 55.

INTERLUDE 5. PUSH ON? MOVE OUT?

1. The Drs. Namie are world experts on workplace bullying, and their books are valuable resources for anyone facing these issues at work. See Gary Namie and Ruth F. Namie, *The Bully-Free Workplace: Stop Jerks, Weasels, and Snakes from Killing Your Organization* (Hoboken, NJ: John Wiley & Sons, 2011); and Gary Namie and Ruth F. Namie, *The Bully at Work: What You Can Do to Stop the Hurt and Reclaim Your Dignity on the Job*, 2nd ed. (Naperville, IL: Sourcebooks, Inc., 2009). The Workplace Bullying Institute, www.workplacebullying.org/the-drs-namie, is another resource.

2. Noel M. Tichy and Warren G. Bennis, *Judgment: How Winning Leaders Make Great Calls* (New York: Penguin, 2009).

3. Richard E. Boyatzis and Annie McKee, *Resonant Leadership: Renewing Yourself and Connecting with Others Through Mindfulness, Hope, and Compassion* (Boston: Harvard Business School Publishing, 2005).

INTERLUDE 6: A SURE TOUR DE FORCE

1. In his classic *Leadership Without Easy Answers* (Cambridge, MA: Harvard University Press, 1998, chapter 6), Ronald Heifetz asserts the importance of "giving the work back to the people." Leaders provide protection, order, and direction; but the adaptive learning necessary for group or organizational change only comes when followers engage, discover, and learn for themselves—and accept the responsibility for doing so. This is especially important when "the application of known methods and procedures will not suffice" (125).

2. Marshall Goldsmith and Mark Reiter, *What Got You Here Won't Get You There: How Successful People Become Even More Successful* (New York: Hyperion, 2007).

EPILOGUE. THE SURE ROUTE TO SUCCESS: ENGAGEMENT

1. www.workplacebullying.org/individuals/problem/being-bullied.

2. www.workplacebullying.org/individuals/impact/physical-health-harm; www.workplacebullying.org/multi/pdf/2011-IP-B.pdf.

3. Amit Sood, *The Mayo Clinic Guide to Stress-Free Living* (Philadelphia: Da Capo Press, 2013),

4. R.D. Richardson, Jr., *William James: In the Maelstrom of American Modernism* (New York: Mariner Books, 2006), 5.

5. The distinction between intention and action—between one's espoused theory and theory in use, in the language of Chris Argyris and Donald Schön—is a landmark set of ideas in both organizational and leadership theory. Important works by the authors developing this distinction include: Chris Argyris, *Increasing Leadership Effectiveness* (New York: John Wiley & Sons, 1976); Chris Argyris, *Teaching Smart People How to Learn*, Harvard Business Review Classics (Boston: Harvard Business School Press, 2008); Chris Argyris and Donald Schön, *Theory*

in Practice: Increasing Professional Effectiveness (San Francisco: Jossey-Bass, 1992); and Donald Schön, *The Reflective Practitioner: How Professionals Think in Action* (New York: Basic Books, 1983).

6. Harold Pinter, *Complete Works 1954–1960*, vol. 1 (New York: Grove Press, 1976), 15.

———

THE SKILLS OF ENGAGEMENT TUTORIAL

1. e. e. cummings, *Introduction to New Poems*. Accessed December 12, 2015 at http://poems.writers-network.com/pdf/article-662.pdf.
2. Warren Berger, *A More Beautiful Question: The Power of Inquiry to Spark Breakthrough Ideas* (New York: Bloomsbury, 2014).
3. Edgar Schein, *Humble Inquiry: The Gentle Art of Asking Instead of Telling* (San Francisco: Berrett-Koehler, 2013).
4. Clayton M. Christensen, *The Innovator's Dilemma: The Revolutionary Book That Will Change the Way You Do Business* (New York: Harper-Business, 2011).
5. Susan Cain, *Quiet: The Power of Introverts in a World That Can't Stop Talking* (New York: Broadway Books, 2013).
6. Alan Alda, *Things I Overheard While Talking to Myself* (New York: Random House, 2008).
7. Lee G. Bolman and Terrence E. Deal, *How Great Leaders Think: The Art of Reframing* (San Francisco: Jossey-Bass/John Wiley & Sons, 2014).
8. Chris Argyris, *Overcoming Organizational Defenses: Facilitating Organizational Learning* (Upper Saddle River, NJ: Prentice-Hall/Pearson Education, 1990). There are many visuals of Argyris's *Ladder of Inference* on the Internet. One accessed December 12, 2015 is https://www.google.com/search?q=ladder+of+inference&biw=1920&bih=946&tbm=isch&imgil=qrKYxAViTNl6zM%253A%253BRJ6YOEwQbvL_RM%253Bhttp%25253A%25252F%25252Fwhatsthepont.com%25252F2015%25252F07%25252F11%25252Fthe-ladder-of-inference-climbing-down-from-expert-bias%25252F&source=iu&pf=m&fir=qrKYxAViTNl6zM%253A%252CRJ6YOEwQbvL_RM%252C_&dpr=1&usg=__gljBP3KguoZsEOT8RnljOIDmpt8%3D&ved=0ahUKEwikq_Wln9fJAhWMez4KHWXTBfkQyjcILg&ei=uI5sVqTvGIz3-QHlppfID

w#imgrc=qrKYxAViTNl6zM%3A&usg=__gljBP3KguoZsEOT8Rnlj
OIDmpt8%3D.

9. Peter Senge, *The Fifth Discipline: The Art and Practice of the Learning* (New York: Doubleday, 2006).

10. http://amorebeautifulquestion.com/einstein-questioning/#jp-carousel-4256.

11. Steven B. Sample, "Thinking Gray and Free," in Joan V. Gallos, ed., *Business Leadership* (San Francisco: Jossey-Bass, 2008).

12. Steven B. Sample, *The Contrarian's Guide to Leadership* (San Francisco: Jossey-Bass/John Wiley & Sons, 2002).

13. Ibid., 13–14.

14. Warren Berger, *A More Beautiful Question: The Power of Inquiry to Spark Breakthrough Ideas* (New York: Bloomsbury, 2014).

15. Steven B. Sample, "Thinking Gray and Free," in Joan V. Gallos, ed., *Business Leadership* (San Francisco: Jossey-Bass, 2008).

16. Sample, *Contrarian's Guide*, 12.

17. Ibid., 13.

18. Amit Sood, *The Mayo Clinic Guide to Stress-free Living* (Boston: Da Capo Press, 2013), Chapters 12, 13, 14.

19. His Holiness the Dalai Lama, *Ethics for the New Millennium* (New York: Riverhead Books/Penguin Putnam, 1999).

20. Sood, *Mayo Clinic Guide*, Chapter 13.

21. William Ury, *The Power of a Positive No: How to Say NO and Still Get to YES* (New York: Bantam, 2007).

22. Kelly Leonard and Tom Yorton, *Yes, And: Lessons from the Second City* (New York: HarperCollins, 2015).

23. Sood, *Mayo Clinic Guide*, 133–145.

24. William A. Kahn, *Holding Fast: The Struggle to Create Resilient Caregiving Organizations* (New York: Brunner-Routledge, 2005).

25. Donald Schön, *Educating the Reflective Practitioner* (San Francisco: Jossey-Bass, 1987), 31.

26. Donald Schön, *The Reflective Practitioner* (New York: Basic, 1983), 68.

27. Mark Doty, *Heaven's Coast: A Memoir* (New York: HarperPerennial, 1996).

28. Louise DeSalvo, *Writing as a Way of Healing: How Telling Our Stories Transforms Our Lives* (Boston: Beacon Press, 1999).

29. Ibid., 8.

30. Ray Bradbury, *Zen in the Art of Writing: Essays on Creativity* (New York: Bantam, 1992).

31. Vivian Gornick, *The Situation and the Story: The Art of Personal Narrative* (New York: Farrar, Straus and Giroux, 2001), 9.

32. Lemony Snicket, *Horseradish* (New York: HarperCollins, 2004).

33. www.workplacebullying.org/individuals/problem/being-bullied.

34. Ellen J. Langer, *The Power of Mindful Learning* (Cambridge, MA: Perseus, 1997).

35. Ibid., 23.

36. Ellen J. Langer, *Mindfulness* (Boston: Da Capo Press, 1989).

37. Langer, *Power of Mindful Learning*, 37.

38. Sood, *Mayo Clinic Guide.*

39. www.brainyquote.com/quotes/quotes/m/muhammadyu462190.html#M QQPLF3V552sIdZT.99.

40. www.apa.org/helpcenter/road-resilience.aspx.

41. Lee G. Bolman and Joan V. Gallos, *Reframing Academic Leadership* (San Francisco: Jossey-Bass/John Wiley & Sons, 2011), chapters 8–13.

42. Amy Morin, *13 Things Mentally Strong People Don't Do: Take Back Your Power, Embrace Change, Face Your Fears, and Training Your Brain for Happiness and Success* (New York: William Morrow, 2014).

43. www.brainyquote.com/quotes/quotes/j/josephcamp384345.html#EVM g81bK02lX6dgw.99.

44. Mihaly Csikszentmyhalyi, *Finding Flow: The Psychology of Engagement with Everyday Life* (New York: Basic Books, 1997).

45. John Whiting, *YoYo Ma: A Biography* (Westport, CT: Greenwood, 2008).

46. Phil Jackson, *Sacred Hoops: Spiritual Lessons of a Hardwood Warrior* (New York: Hyperion, 2006).

47. See Sood, *Mayo Clinic Guide*, chapters 2, 5, 6, 7.

48. Matthew Killingsworth and Daniel Gilbert, "A Wandering Mind Is an Unhappy Mind," *Science* (2010): 330–932.

49. Donald Hebb, as quoted in Sood, *Mayo Clinic Guide*, 10. Hebb is the father of neuroscience, and *American Psychologist* named him one of the twentieth century's most eminent and influential theorists in the realm of brain function and behavior.

50. Sood, *Mayo Clinic Guide*, 66.

51. www.brainyquote.com/quotes/quotes/d/davidsuzuk193053.html#sJ0w UIyu7rw8cecT.99.

52. As examples, see A. P. de Geus, "Planning as Learning," *Harvard Business Review* (March–April 1991) and P. Schwartz, *The Art of the Long View* (New York: Doubleday, 1991).

53. L. Heracleous and C. D. Jacobs, "Developing Strategy: The Serious Business of Play," in Joan V. Gallos (ed.), *Business Leadership* (San Francisco: Jossey-Bass, 2008).

54. Bernie S. Siegel, *Prescription for Living* (New York: HarperCollins, 1998).

55. Daniel H. Pink, *A Whole New Mind: Why Right-Brainers Will Rule the Future* (New York: Riverhead Books, 2006).

56. Fabio Sala, "Laughing All the Way to the Bank," *Harvard Business Review* (September 2003).

57. Lee G. Bolman and Terrence E. Deal, *Reframing Organizations: Artistry, Choice, and Leadership*, 4th ed. (San Francisco: Jossey-Bass/John Wiley & Sons, 2008).

58. James G. March, "The Technology of Foolishness," in J. G. March and J. Olsen (eds.), *Ambiguity and Choice in Organizations* (Bergen, Norway: Universitetsforlaget, 1976).

59. Sood, *Mayo Clinic Guide*, 243.

60. Pink, *A Whole New Mind*, 209–215.

61. www.laughteryoga.org/english/laughteryoga.

62. William R. Noonan, *Discussing the Undiscussable: A Guide to Overcoming Defensive Routines in the Workplace* (San Francisco: Jossey-Bass/John Wiley & Sons, 2007).

63. Roger Fisher and William Ury, *Getting to Yes: Negotiating Agreement without Giving In* (New York: Penguin, 1991).

64. Drea Zigarmi, Susan Fowler, Patricia Zigarmi, and Ken Blanchard, "Giving Feedback: Participant Workbook" 2015. Accessed December 12, 2015 at https://www.kenblanchard.com/getattachment/Solutions/By-Offering/Skill-Training-Modules/Giving-Feedback/Giving-Feedback-PW-Look-Inside.pdf.

65. Ibid.

ACKNOWLEDGMENTS

WE HAVE BEEN HELPED BY FAR MORE PEOPLE than we will ever succeed in acknowledging. We are blessed with a large circle of remarkable friends and colleagues, and they have taught us much. We begin with Terry Deal, a valued teacher, wonderful collaborator, and beloved friend to us both. Equally significant is the late Chris Argyris, an extraordinary teacher and friend who was instrumental in both our decisions to make a career of studying organizations and leadership. Our first-born is named Chris, so no more need be said about the place that Chris holds in our hearts. Ed Schein is also at the top of our list for his friendship, keen ability to cut through complexity, and impact on us and so many others. Other highly valued individuals have enriched our lives and careers in important ways; and we send special nods of affection and appreciation to Dave Brown, Marcy Crary, Tim Hall, Mary Jo Hatch, Todd Jick, Bill Kahn, Leslie Kagan, Diane Kellogg, Clancy Martin, Bob Marx, Phil Mirvis, Ann Olivarius, Barry and Karen Oshry, Amy Sales, Lorie Spencer, and our cultured and artsy Mahkeenac Heights neighbors (especially Joel Laski, Lloyd Johnson, John "Ace" McCarthy, and Linda and David Burghardt).

We have learned from and tested many of our ideas with our colleagues and students over the years at the University of Missouri-Kansas City, Harvard, Babson, Princeton, Carnegie Mellon, UMass-Boston, Yale, and Wheelock, as well as with participants in many workshops, corporate programs, and institutes across the world. We are particularly grateful to the many participants we have taught in summer leadership programs under the auspices of the Harvard

Institutes for Higher Education. These talented leaders trusted us with their professional stories and challenges, some of which are reflected in this book.

Working effectively with difficult people is a lot easier to study than to do, and we are grateful to a number of special individuals who gave us an opportunity to practice and develop our abilities to understand and cope with people whom we found really, really, difficult. For their protection (and on the advice of counsel), we won't name them all here, but acknowledge the benefits of being so up-close and personal in studying these perennial and powerful dynamics. We approach the publication of this book the same way we began the project: fired with enthusiasm in the search for new ways to bring health and sanity to troubled organizations and relationships.

We have been hanging around Jossey-Bass/John Wiley & Sons for so long that it feels like family—but, like many families and the rest of the publishing industry, a family that has been seeing a lot of change. Our original editor for this project, Kathe Sweeney, has moved on to the exciting world of online learning. We are grateful for Kathe's early support of this and on our other published works; and we are pleased to call her our dear friend. Happily, we are also blessed with a terrific successor in Jeanenne Ray, who has shepherded this book to publication. We're grateful to many others at Jossey-Bass/Wiley for their high level of support and professionalism, including Heather Brosius and Lauren Freestone.

Finally, we thank our family. Our two sons, Brad and Chris, are talented young men who enrich our lives. We love them, and we're deeply proud of them both. Chris has transitioned from Wall Street to solar energy to leadership in online marketing, and along the way has become a serial entrepreneur and a prolific author in his own right. Brad deserves a special nod as the last in the roost and the child most likely to pursue his own academic career. Just out of college, Brad has already accumulated publications and international conference appearances, and is heading on in search of a PhD. Lee's other children contribute their own brands of artistry and grace to the family. Theater, music, teaching, arts management, and our Massachusetts grandchild, Foster, fill the lives of Shelley and Christine Woodberry. Scott Bolman is the jet-setting, international lighting designer extraordinaire and a keeper of the family backpacking tradition. Lori and Barry Holwegner anchor the Western contingent and take good care of granddaughter Jazmyne. Edward Bolman and son James, who is now thriving among the Banana Slugs at the University of California/Santa Cruz, round out the pack.

Our parents, Elizabeth and John Gallos and Florence and Eldred Bolman are no longer with us, but we know they would have been tickled to see this joint venture and themselves saluted in it. We honor their encouragement and support—and love of learning that we hope we have passed along to our children—by adding our appreciation and affection here.

Finally, we continue our tradition of giving a nod to some wayward canine who has served as a loyal distraction from writer's block. This book's award goes to the gorgeous yet impish, perennially hungry, always difficult, mega-cockapoo, Douglas McGregor. Family life in all its richness is grand!

Our first attempt to write together decades ago resulted in an unpublished manuscript that still lies buried in a file drawer somewhere. We waited a while before again testing whether book-writing and a viable marriage are remotely compatible. But our next effort produced a well-received book on academic leadership, published in 2011, that we're very proud of. It gave us the encouragement to try again. We take pride in all that we've been able to do together, and we reaffirm our love and commitment to each other, our shared interests, and our belief in the possibilities for a more just and equitable world. Onward!

ABOUT THE AUTHORS

LEE G. BOLMAN holds the Marion Bloch/Missouri Chair in Leadership at the Henry W. Bloch School of Management at the University of Missouri–Kansas City, where he has also served as department chair and interim dean. He holds a BA in History and a PhD in Organizational Behavior from Yale University.

Bolman consults and lectures worldwide to corporations, public agencies, universities, and schools. Prior to assuming his current position, he taught at Carnegie Mellon and then for more than 20 years at the Harvard Graduate School of Education, where he served as director and principal investigator for the National Center for Educational Leadership and for the Harvard School Leadership Academy. He also served as educational chair for two Harvard executive programs—the Institute for Educational Management (IEM) and the Management Development Program (MDP)—and was the founder of MDP.

Bolman has written numerous books on leadership and organizations with coauthor Terrence E. Deal, including *How Great Leaders Think: The Art of Reframing* (2014); *Reframing Organizations: Artistry, Choice, and Leadership* (5th edition, 2013); *Leading with Soul: an Uncommon Journey of Spirit* (3rd edition, 2011); *Reframing the Path to School Leadership: A Guide for Principals and Teachers* (2nd edition, 2010); *The Wizard and the Warrior: Leading with Passion and Power* (2006); *Escape from Cluelessness: a Guide for the Organizationally-Challenged* (2000); *Becoming a Teacher Leader* (1993); and *Modern Approaches to Understanding and Managing Organizations* (1984). He is also coauthor with Joan V. Gallos of *Reframing*

Academic Leadership (2011). Bolman's books have been translated into more than 10 languages; and his other publications include numerous cases, chapters, and articles in scholarly and professional journals.

In 2003, Bolman received the David L. Bradford Outstanding Educator Award from the Organizational Behavior Teaching Society for his lifetime contributions to teaching and learning in the organizational sciences.

JOAN V. GALLOS is currently Professor of Leadership at Wheelock College, where she also served as Vice President for Academic Affairs. She holds a bachelor's degree *cum laude* in English from Princeton, and master's and doctoral degrees in Organizational Behavior and Professional Education from the Harvard Graduate School of Education.

Prior to Wheelock, Gallos was University of Missouri Curators' Distinguished Teaching Professor and Director of the Executive MBA program at the Henry W. Bloch School of Management at the University of Missouri–Kansas City, where she had also served as tenured Professor and Dean of Education, Coordinator of University Accreditation, Special Assistant to the Chancellor for Strategic Planning, and Director of the Higher Education Graduate Programs. In addition to her academic appointments at Wheelock and UMKC, Gallos has taught at the Radcliffe Seminars, Harvard Graduate School of Education, University of Massachusetts–Boston, and Babson College, as well as in executive programs at a variety of institutions.

Gallos has published widely on professional effectiveness, organizational change, and leadership. She is coauthor with Lee G. Bolman of *Reframing Academic Leadership* (2011); editor of *Organization Development* (2006) and of *Business Leadership* (2nd edition, 2008); coauthor with V. Jean Ramsey of *Teaching Diversity: Listening to the Soul, Speaking from the Heart* (1997); creator of a variety of published management education teaching and training materials, including the instructional guides for the *Jossey-Bass Reader* series in management; and author of numerous articles and chapters in scholarly and professional journals. She has also coauthored a play on teen health; drafted a fantasy book for young readers and a children's book on friendship; and is hard at work on her first adult novel (and TV mini-series based on it).

She has served as the editor-in-chief of the *Journal of Management Education*; as a Salzburg Seminar Fellow; as president of the Organizational Behavior Teaching Society; and on a number of national and regional advisory councils and nonprofit boards, including as a founding board member for Actors Theater of Kansas City and for the Kansas City Library Foundation and as a current member of the New Rep Theater board at the Arsenal Center for the Performing Arts in Watertown, MA.

Gallos has received numerous awards for writing, teaching, and service, including both the *Sage of the Society* and the *Distinguished Service* awards from the Organizational Behavior Teaching Society; the *Fritz Roethlisberger Memorial Award* for the best article on management education (and was finalist for the same prize in subsequent years); and the Radcliffe College/Harvard University *Excellence in Teaching* award. She proudly served as the designer and Founding Director of the Truman Center for the Healing Arts, based in Kansas City's public teaching hospital, which received the 2004 Kansas City Business Committee for the Arts Partnership Award as the best partnership between a large organization and the arts.

Joan Gallos and Lee Bolman have worked together for almost 40 years on a variety of teaching, training, and consulting projects for universities, corporations, nonprofits, and government agencies. This is their second book together.

INDEX